GIANT BOOK OF

MENSA
MIND
CHALLENGES

EDITED BY TODD JOHNSON, WITH PUZZLES BY:

**J.J. MENDOZA FERNÁNDEZ, JAIME & LEA PONIACHIK,
KAREN RICHARDS, TIM SOLE & ROD MARSHALL**

STERLING INNOVATION
An imprint of Sterling Publishing Co., Inc.

New York / London
www.sterlingpublishing.com

Material in this collection was adapted from:
Quick-to-Solve Brainteasers © 1998 J.J. Mendoza Fernández
Hard-to-Solve Brainteasers © 1998 Jaime & Lea Poniachik
Nearly Impossible Brain Bafflers © 1998 Tim Sole & Rod Marshall
Mighty Mini Mind Bogglers © 1999 Karen C. Richards

2   4   6   8   10   9   7   5   3   1

This edition published by Sterling Publishing Co., Inc. in 2008
387 Park Avenue South, New York, NY 10016
© 2003 by Sterling Publishing Co., Inc.
Distributed in Canada by Sterling Publishing
c/o Canadian Manda Group, 165 Dufferin Street
Toronto, Ontario, Canada M6K 3H6
Distributed in Great Britain by GMC Distribution Services
Castle Place, 166 High Street, Lewes, East Sussex, England BN7 1XU
Distributed in Australia by Capricorn Link (Australia) Pty. Ltd.
P.O. Box 704, Windsor, NSW 2756, Australia

Sterling ISBN-13: 978-1-4027-5989-5
ISBN-10: 1-4027-5989-4

For information about custom editions, special sales, premium and
corporate purchases, please contact Sterling Special Sales Department
at 800-805-5489 or specialsales@sterlingpublishing.com.

Quick-to-Solve
BRAIN
TEASERS

This section contains many different types of puzzles: numerical puzzles, logic puzzles, word games, lateral thinking puzzles, riddles, etc. Most of them are extremely short and can be solved mentally in just a minute or two. When writing is required, a small slip of paper should be more than adequate.

The purpose of these puzzles is to entertain. The correct answer is not always obvious. The reader will notice that the puzzles are often misleading or involve humor in the answer. Therefore, use your imagination, be alert, and have an open mind when trying the puzzles.

The answers for this section can be found on pages 59 through 83.

NUMBERS

1234567890

1

How many times can you subtract 6 from 30?

2

What number can you subtract half from to obtain a result that is 0?

3

How can half of 12 be 7?

4

Find two positive numbers that have a one-digit answer when multiplied and a two-digit answer when added.

5

Find two whole, positive numbers that have the same answer when multiplied together as when one is divided by the other.

6

Find two positive numbers that have the same answer when multiplied together as when added together.

7

Find a two-digit number that equals two times the result of multiplying its digits.

8

Find three whole, positive numbers that have the same answer when multiplied together as when added together.

9

What two two-digit numbers are each equal to their right-most digit squared?

10

Find the highest number that can be written with three digits.

COMPARING NUMBERS

11

The ages of a father and a son add up to 55. The father's age is the son's age reversed. How old are they?

12

How much do ten pieces of candy cost if one thousand pieces cost $10?

13

An outlet and a lightbulb cost $1.20. We know that the outlet costs $1 more than the lightbulb. How much does each cost?

PERCENTAGES

14

If 75% of all women are tall, 75% are brunette, and 75% are pretty, what is the minimum percentage of tall, brunette, pretty women?

15

32 students took a nationwide exam and all the students from New York passed it. If the students from New York made up exactly 5% of the total number of the students that passed the test, how many students passed it and how many students were from New York?

16

Of the 960 people in a theater, 17% tipped 5¢ to the usher, 50% of the remaining 83% tipped 10¢, and the rest tipped nothing. How much did the usher get?

OTHER NUMBERS

17

What must you do to make the equation below true?
81 x 9 = 801.

18

There are 100 buildings along a street. A sign maker is ordered to number the buildings from 1 to 100. How many "9's" will he need?

19

How many tickets with different points of origination and destination can be sold on a bus line that travels a loop of 25 stops?

20

We know that humans have up to 100,000 hairs. In a city with more than 200,000 people, would it be possible to find two or more people with the same number of hairs?

COUNTING

21

All my ties are red except two. All my ties are blue except two. All my ties are brown except two. How many ties do I have?

22

A street that's 30 yards long has a chestnut tree every six yards on both sides. How many chestnut trees are on the entire street?

23

A pet shop owner is in the countryside. If he says, "one bird per olive tree," there is one bird too many. However, if he says, "two birds per olive tree," there are no birds left over. How many birds and olive trees are there?

24

In a singles tennis tournament, 111 players participated. They used a new ball for each match. When a player lost one match, he was eliminated from the tournament. How many balls did they need?

25

Peter and John had a picnic. Peter had already eaten half of the muffins when John ate half of the remaining muffins plus three more. There were no muffins left. How many muffins did they take to the picnic?

26

A shepherd says to another, "If I give you one sheep, you will have twice the number of sheep that I have, but if you give me one, we will both have the same number of sheep." How many sheep does each shepherd have?

27

If I put in one canary per cage, I have one bird too many. However, if I put in two canaries per cage, I have one cage too many. How many cages and birds do I have?

28

If 1½ sardines cost 1½ dollars, how much would 7½ sardines cost?

29

If a brick weighs 3 pounds plus ½ a brick, what's the weight of 1½ bricks?

30

If 1½ dozen sardines costs 9½ dollars, how much do 18 sardines cost?

31

If 1½ men can eat 1½ pies in 1½ minutes, how many pies can 3 men eat in half an hour?

32

Yesterday afternoon, I went to visit my friend Albert, who is a painter. While I was watching him paint, I told him, "No wonder it takes you so long to finish a painting. Since I arrived, you have entered the studio twelve times." How many times did he leave the studio?

33

If two ducks are swimming in front of another duck, two ducks are swimming behind another duck, and one duck is swimming between two other ducks, what is the minimum number of ducks?

34

Two people are flipping coins. Each time, they bet $1 apiece. At the end, one person won $3 and the other one won three times. How many games did they play?

MEASURING TIME, VOLUME, LENGTH, ETC.

35

A bottle with a cylindrical shape at the bottom and with an irregular shape at the top is filled halfway to the top with liquid. The cylindrical part contains approximately three-fourths of the capacity of the bottle and we wish to determine the exact percentage of liquid that the bottle contains. We cannot open it and we can only use a ruler.
What must we do?

36

If one nickel is worth 5¢, how much is half of one half of a nickel worth?

37

Two soldiers have been ordered to do the following chores:
    1. Peel potatoes.
    2. Do the dishes.
    3. Mow the lawn.
Each of these chores, when done by one person, takes one hour. If they start at 8 a.m., what could they do to take as little time as possible if they have only one knife, one lawn mower, and one sink with room for one person?

38

A spider spins its web in a window frame. Each day, it spins an area equal to that of the amount already completed. It takes 30 days to cover the entire window frame. How long would two spiders take? (In the case of the two spiders, each of them spins an amount equal to the area of the existing part of the web made by that particular spider.)

39

We put a spore in a test tube. Every hour the spore divides into three parts, all the same size as the original part. If we put it in at 3 p.m., at 9 p.m. the tube will be completely full. At what time will the tube be one-third full?

40

How long is a rope that is two yards shorter than another rope that is three times the length of the first rope?

41

If a post is six yards longer than half of its own length, how long is the post?

42

How much mud (measured in liters) is there in a rectangular hole two meters wide, three meters long, and three meters deep?

43

One mother gave 25 books to her daughter and another mother gave her daughter 8 books. However, between both daughters they only increased their collection by 25 books. How can this be?

COMPARING TIME, VOLUME, LENGTH, ETC.

44

Emily is taller than Ann and shorter than Dolores. Who is the tallest of the three?

45

Rose is now as old as Joan was six years ago. Who is older?

46

If Emily speaks in a softer voice than Ann, and Dolores in a louder voice than Ann, does Emily speak louder or softer than Dolores?

47

James is sitting between John and Peter. Philip is sitting on Peter's right. Between whom is Peter sitting?

48

What has more value, one pound of $10 gold coins or half a pound of $20 gold coins?

49

A man went into a store and bought an umbrella for $10. He gave the salesperson a $50 bill. The salesperson went to the bank to get change. Two hours later, the bank teller went to the store claiming that the $50 bill was counterfeit, so the salesperson had to exchange it for a real one with the bank teller. Between the customer and the bank, how much did the store lose?

50

We have two pitchers, one with one quart of water and the other with one quart of wine. We take a tablespoon of the wine and mix it in the pitcher of water. Then we take a tablespoon from this pitcher and mix it into the pitcher with the wine. Is there more wine in the water pitcher or more water in the wine pitcher? What would have happened if after pouring a spoonful of wine into the water, we had not mixed it well?

51

A sultan wanted to offer his daughter in marriage to the candidate whose horse would win the race. However, the rules of the race stated that the winner would be the one in last place. He didn't want the race to last forever, so he thought of a way to solve this. What was it?

 WEIGHTS

52

On one side of a scale we have a partially filled fishbowl. When we put a fish in the bowl, the total weight of the bowl increases by exactly the same as the weight of the fish. However, if we hold the fish by the tail and partially introduce it into the water, will the total weight be greater than before introducing the fish?

53

We have a scale and a set of weights in a field. The scale is not very accurate, but it is consistent in its inaccuracies. How can we know the exact weight of four apples?

54

A little bird weighing five ounces is sleeping in a cage. We put the cage on a scale and it weighs one pound. The bird then wakes up and starts flying all over the cage. What will the scale indicate while the bird is in the air?

55

We have ten sacks full of balls. All sacks contain balls weighing ten ounces each, except one of the sacks, which contains balls weighing nine ounces each. By weighing the balls, what would be the minimum number of weighings required (on a scale that gives weight readouts) to identify the sack containing the defective balls?

56

Now we have ten sacks that contain either ten-ounce balls or nine-ounce balls. Each sack has at least 1,000 balls, and all the balls in one sack are the same weight. However, we do not know how many sacks contain the nine-ounce balls or which ones they are. How can we identify these sacks by weighing the balls (on a scale that gives weight readouts) in the fewest number of tries?

CHAINS

57

I have six pieces of a chain, each piece made up of four links, and I want to make a single straight chain out of them. The blacksmith charges 10¢ for cutting each link and 50¢ for welding a link. How much will the chain cost?

58

A lady arrives at a hotel where rooms are $10 per night. When she checks in, she does not have enough money, but she offers to pay with a clasped gold bracelet. The bracelet has seven links, each valued at $10. What would be the fewest number of cuts necessary to let her stay for one week if she wants to pay one day at a time?

59

"And then I took out my sword and cut the thick chain that was linked to two posts into two pieces," said the samurai.

"That is not true," said the monk.

How did the monk know the samurai's story was untrue?

MIXING

60

We have ten glasses sitting in a row. The first five are filled with water and the other five are empty. What would be the minimum number of glasses needed to move so that the full and the empty glasses alternate?

61

In five plastic cups there are five marbles, each of different colors: white, black, red, green, and blue. We mark each cup randomly with the initial of one of the colors. If the white, green, red, and blue marbles are in their respective cups, how likely is it that the black marble is in its cup?

62

We have eight pairs of white socks and ten pairs of black socks in a box. What would be the minimum number of socks that we need to take out of the box to ensure that we get one pair of the same color? (Imagine that you cannot see the color when you are picking them from the box.)

63

We have 8 pairs of white socks, 9 pairs of black socks, and 11 pairs of blue socks in a box. What would be the minimum number of socks that we need to take out of the box to ensure that we get one pair of the same color? (Imagine that you cannot see the color when you are picking them from the box.)

64

We have six pairs of white gloves and six pairs of black gloves in a box. What would be the minimum number of gloves that we need to take out of the box to ensure that we get one pair? (Imagine that you cannot see the color when you are picking them from the box.)

65

We have six white marbles, four black marbles, and one red marble in a box. What would be the least number of marbles that we need to take out of the box to ensure that we get three of the same color?

66

Distribute ten marbles in three plastic cups so that every cup contains an odd number of marbles. You must use all ten.

67

Distribute nine marbles in four boxes so that each box contains an odd number of marbles, different from the three other boxes. You must use all nine.

68

We have three boxes. One contains two black marbles, the second box contains two white marbles, and the third box contains one black and one white marble. The boxes are marked BB, WW, and BW. However, no code corresponds with the marbles in its box. What would be the least number of marbles that must be randomly picked, from one or several boxes, to identify their contents?

CLOCKS

69

A schoolteacher uses a five-hour hourglass to keep track of class time. One day, he sets the hourglass at 9 a.m., and while he is teaching his class, a student inadvertently inverts the hourglass. Another student, who notices this, sets the hourglass to its initial position at 11:30 a.m. In this way, the class ends at 3 p.m. At what time did the first student invert the hourglass?

70

A clock gains half a minute every day. Another clock doesn't work. Which one will show the correct time more often?

71

What time is it when a clock strikes 13 times?

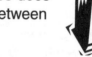

72

In a conventional clock, how many times does the minute hand pass the hour hand between noon and midnight?

73

If a clock takes two seconds to strike two o'clock, how long will it take to strike three o'clock?

74

When I gave Albert a ride home, I noticed that the clock in his living room took seven seconds to strike eight o'clock. I immediately asked him, "How long do I have to wait to hear it strike twelve o'clock?"

75

A clock takes five seconds when striking six o'clock. How long will it take when striking twelve o'clock?

CALENDAR

76

A Roman was born the first day of the thirtieth year before Christ and died the first day of the thirtieth year after Christ. How many years did he live?

77

On March 15, a friend was telling me, "Every day I have a cup of coffee. I drank thirty-one cups in January, twenty-eight in February, and fifteen in March. So far, I drank seventy-four cups of coffee. Do you know how many cups of coffee I would have drunk thus far if it had been a leap year?"

78

If yesterday had been Wednesday's tomorrow and tomorrow is Sunday's yesterday, what day would today be?

79

Mrs. Smith left on a trip the day after the day before yesterday and she will be back the eve of the day after tomorrow. How many days is she away?

80

A man was telling me on a particular occasion, "The day before yesterday I was 35 years old and next year I will turn 38." How can this be?

81

A famous composer blew out 18 candles on his birthday cake and then died less than nine months later. He was 76 at the time of his death and had composed *The Barber of Seville*. How could this happen?

WORDS

82

Find a commonly used word that ends in "t," contains the letters "ven," and starts with "in."

83

If you can speak properly, you will be able to answer the following question. Which is correct, "The yolk of an egg is white" or "The yolk of an egg are white"?

84

What is the opposite of "I AM NOT LEAVING"?

85

What 11-letter word is pronounced incorrectly by more than 99% of Ivy League graduates?

86

What seven-letter word becomes longer when the third letter is removed?

87

Five times four twenty, plus two, equals twenty-three. Is this true?

88

Paris starts with a "p" and ends with an "e". Is this true?

89

A phone conversation:

"May I speak to the director?"
"Who's calling?"
"John Rominch."
"I beg your pardon. Could you spell your last name?"
"R as in Rome, O as in Oslo, M as in Madrid, I as in Innsbruck..."
"I as in what?"

"Innsbruck."

"Thanks. Please go ahead."

"N as in Nome . . ."

This does not make sense. Why?

90

What can you always find in the middle of a taxicab?

91

Is the sentence "This statement is false" true or false?

92

What occurs once in June and twice in August, but never occurs in October?

93

"I must admit that I was not serious when I was telling you that I was not kidding about rethinking my decision of not changing my mind," my friend was telling me. So, is he really going to change his mind or not?

94

A criminal is sentenced to death. Before his execution, he is allowed to make a statement. If his statement is false, he will be hanged, and if his statement is true, he will be drowned. What should he say to confuse the jury and thus save his life?

COUNTING RELATIVES

95

A woman has five children and half of them are male. Is this possible?

96

A friend was telling me, "I have eight sons and each has one sister." In total, how many children does my friend have?

97

Ann's brother has one more brother than sisters. How many more brothers than sisters does Ann have?

98

I have as many brothers as sisters, but my brothers have twice the number of sisters as brothers. How many of us are there?

FAMILY TIES

99

A doctor has a brother who is an attorney in Alabama, but the attorney in Alabama does not have a brother who is a doctor. How can this be?

100

John wonders, "If Raymond's biological son is my biological son's biological father, how am I related to Raymond?"

101

If your uncle's sister is related to you, but is not your aunt, what is the relation?

102

A group of paleontologists found a prehistoric cave and one of them is congratulated by a biological younger son, who writes a telegram to his biological dad explaining the discovery. Who discovered the cave?

103

The other day, I heard the following conversation:
"Charles is related to you the same way I am to your son."
"And you are related to me in the same way Charles is to you."
How are Charles and the second man related?

104

Can someone marry his brother's wife's mother-in-law?

105

Ann is looking at the portrait of a gentleman. "He is not my father, but his mother was my mother's mother-in-law," she says. Who is this gentleman?

106

Do you know if the Catholic Church allows a man to marry his widow's sister?

107

A friend of mine was looking at a photo when she said, "Brothers and sisters? I have one. And this man's father is my father's son." Who was in the photo?

108

A friend of mine was looking at a photo when he said, "Brothers and sisters? I have none. But this man's son is my father's son." Who was in the photo?

109

Two women are talking on the street. When they see two men coming, they say, "There are our fathers, our mother's husbands, our children's fathers, and our own husbands." How can you explain this?

QUICK LOGIC

110

What was the biggest ocean in the world before Balboa discovered the Pacific Ocean?

111

How many cookies could you eat on an empty stomach?

112

Three mature and hefty women were walking in San Francisco under one regular-size umbrella. Why didn't they get wet?

113

What can a pitcher be filled with so it is lighter than when it is full of air?

114

A dog is tied to a 15-foot-long leash. How can the dog reach a bone that is 20 feet away?

115

I went into a store and found out that it cost $3 for 400, which meant that each part cost $1. What did I want to buy?

116

Last week, my uncle Peter was able to turn his bedroom light off and get into bed before the room was dark. The light switch and the bed are ten feet apart. How did he accomplish this?

117

How can you make 30¢ with only two coins if one of the coins is not a nickel?

118

The only barber in my town likes foreigners to go into his shop. Last week, he was telling me, "The truth is that I'd rather give two foreigners haircuts than to give a haircut to one person in town." What was the logic behind this?

119

My brother Mark says he is able to place a bottle in the middle of a room and by crawling on the floor, he can slide into it. How can this be?

120

Last Friday I flew to San Diego. It was a scary flight. About an hour after getting onto the plane, I saw a very thick fog and then the engines stopped due to lack of fuel. Why didn't we die?

121

While eating out, my brother-in-law Paul found a fly in his coffee. After taking the cup away, the waiter came back with a different cup of coffee. My brother-in-law got upset and returned it, saying that the coffee in the second cup was the same as in the first one. How did he know?

122

You find shelter in a mountain lodge on a windy night. When you go in, you only find a match, a candle, a sheet of newspaper, and a torch. You need to light the fireplace. What would you light first?

123

A mother has six children and five potatoes. How can she feed each an equal amount of pototoes? (Do not use fractions.)

124

The giraffe and its offspring are walking in a field. The little giraffe tells a friend, "I am the daughter of this giraffe, although this giraffe is not my mother." How can you explain this?

125

A farmer has twenty sheep, ten pigs, and ten cows.
If we call the pigs cows, how many cows will he have?

126

Where must a referee be to blow the whistle?

127

In the event of an emergency, can a Muslim baptize a Catholic?

128

It occurs once in a minute, twice in a week, and once in a year. What is it?

129

One night, when my uncle Emil was reading a book
in the living room, his wife turned off the light
and the living room became completely dark.
However, my uncle continued reading.
How is this possible?

130

A man says, "I am going to drink water because I don't have water. If I had it, I would drink wine." What does he do for a living?

131

Imagine you are a taxi driver and you are driving a 1978 yellow cab. Your passengers are an older couple, and they want to travel six miles. You are driving at 40 miles per hour with the tank one-third full, when, two miles into the trip, the tank is down to one-quarter full. Ten minutes later, the trip is over. What is the name and age of the cab driver?

132

A railway line has a double track, except in a tunnel where there is no room for a double track. A train goes into the tunnel in one direction, and another one enters in the opposite direction. Both trains are traveling fast. However, they do not crash. Why?

133

My son was telling me yesterday, "Four days ago, my school's soccer team won a game 4 to 1, although none of the boys on my school's team scored any goals. Also, the other team didn't score against itself accidently." How can this be?

134

Last Thursday, my aunt Martha forgot her driver's license at home. She was traveling down a one-way street in the wrong direction and did not stop at an intersection to let pedestrians go. A policeman was watching her, but did not give her a ticket. Why?

135

Three friends went out for drinks. The waiter brought them a check for $30, so each one of them paid $10. When the waiter took the cash, he realized he had made a mistake, and the check was for $25 instead. When he gave their change back, each friend got $1 and they left the remaining $2 as a tip. Therefore, each customer paid $9; multiplied by three this equals $27; plus $2 for the tip equals $29. Where is the remaining dollar?

136

A 16-year-old boy was driving a moped down a one-way street in the wrong direction. A policeman stopped him and gave him a ticket. The policeman paid the ticket himself. Can you find a logical explanation for this?

137

The butcher, his daughter, the fisherman, and his wife won the lottery and divided the prize into three. How can this be?

138

My friend Albert the butcher wears a size 13 shoe, is six feet tall, and wears a 42-long suit. What does he weigh?

139

There are five apples in one basket and five people in a room. How can you distribute the apples so that each person receives one and there is one apple left in the basket?

140

A man is doing his work. He knows that if his suit tears, he will die. Can you guess his job?

141

We have just invented two words: to sint and to sant. You cannot sint or sant in the street or in the office. You can do both things in the bathroom, in the swimming pool, and at the beach, but in the swimming pool and at the beach you cannot sint completely. You cannot sint without clothes on and you need little or no clothing to sant. Can you guess what the words mean?

142

My cousin Henry can guess the score of a soccer game before the game begins. How can that be?

143

Before my husband left on a trip, he left me $150 in cash and a $500 check. However, when I went to a bank to cash the check, I found out that the account only had $450. How could I cash the check?

144

A bus stops three times during the ride. The ticket costs 12¢ to the first stop, 21¢ to the second stop, and 25¢ to the third stop. A man gets on at the start of the route and gives the driver 25¢. Without talking to the passenger, the driver gives him a ticket to the last stop. How did the driver know?

145

You've probably heard the expression "two's company and three's a crowd." But what's the simplest way to describe four and five?

146

Mary, riding her white horse, decides to go into the forest. How far can she go?

147

What animal eats with its tail?

148

How can you light a match under water?

149

What three shapes can a saber have for it to fit in a sheath?

150

"This parrot can repeat anything it hears," the owner of the pet shop told Janice last week. So my sister bought it. Yesterday she went to return it, claiming that the parrot had not even said one word. However, the pet shop owner had not lied to her. Can you explain this?

151

A man and his son were in a car accident. The boy had a fracture and injuries to one leg and was taken to a nearby hospital in an ambulance. When he was in the operating room, the surgeon said, "I cannot operate on him! He is my son!" Explain this.

152

Why do black sheep eat less grass than white sheep?

LOGIC

153

My cousin Mary dropped an earring in her coffee, but the earring did not get wet. How could this be?

154

I have a book where the foreword comes after the epilogue, the end is in the first half of the book, and the index comes before the introduction. What book is it?

155

How can you explain that one lady works alone as a bartender, yet there is a COUPLE that works behind the counter?

156

My uncle Raphael bought a coin in the flea market for $10. The coin has the head of Emperor Augustus and is dated 27 B.C. The other side is illegible. It is a fake, however. What proves that it is not a true ancient Roman coin?

157

An Air France plane crashes along the border of Portugal and Spain. Rescue teams from both countries are called to the site of the crash to help the victims. In which country do you think the survivors will be buried?

158

The director of a large company asks the security guard working the night shift to call him a cab, because he needs to take a red-eye flight to New York. The guard tells him not to board the plane, because he has just had a dream that the director would have an accident. To be safe, the director decides to wait until the next morning. During the trip, he reads in the paper that the red-eye flight had crashed. When he returns from his trip, he thanks the guard and gives him a bonus. Then he fires him. Why did he fire him?

159

My cousin Edward got soaked while he was walking on the street yesterday. He did not have an umbrella or a hat, so when he got home, his clothes were completely wet. However, not a hair on his head got wet. Why?

160

My sister Sophie lives on the 28th floor of a 32-story building. When my aunt Emily visits her, she takes the elevator to the 25th floor and then walks up the stairs. On her way down, she takes the elevator at the 28th floor all the way down to the ground floor. Why does she do this?

161

A man was sleeping in a hotel. In the middle of the night, he woke up and could not go back to sleep. He picked up the phone and called someone. As soon as he hung up, he fell sound asleep. He did not know the person he was calling. Why did he call that person?

162

When he goes to the bathroom, a man does not know if the hot water faucet is the one on the left or on the right. What does he need to do to be sure that he does not turn on the cold water before he turns on the hot water?

163

A man took his wife to the emergency room. The doctor decided to operate on her immediately. He told the husband that whether the wife died during the operation or survived, he would charge $1,000. The woman did not survive the operation. The husband did not pay anything. Why not?

164

The brothers Albert, Ben, Carl, and Don wear shirt sizes 37, 38, 39, and 40, respectively. Their mother bought one blue shirt for each one of them and embroidered their first initials on the left side. She placed three initials correctly. How many different ways can this happen?

165

If the date of the last Saturday of last month and the first Sunday of this month do not add up to 33, what month are we in?

166

The priest in my hometown announced last year that on a particular day he would walk on water for half an hour. The river was not dry and we could all see that the priest was actually able to walk on water. How did he manage?

167

Two miners go home after work. One of them has his face covered with soot and the other has a clean face. The one with a clean face wipes it with a handkerchief and the one with the dirty face does not do anything. Why?

168

What is there in the middle of a cigar?

169

A remote town has two hair salons. The first one has a dirty mirror, and a floor covered with hair, and the hairdresser has an awful haircut. In the second one, the mirror and floor are very clean and the hairdresser has a great haircut. Where would you go and why?

170

A man ordered a glass of white wine and a glass of red wine at a bar. He took the glass of white wine in his right hand and the one with red in his left hand and drank both. He paid and left. The next day, he did the same. When he was leaving, the waiter said to him:

"I did not know that firemen drank that way."

The man smiled and left. How did the waiter know that he was a fireman?

171

Three meteorologists left a meeting in the middle of the night, during a heavy rain.

"The weather will remain like this until the next full moon," said one of them.

"I agree. And ninety-six hours from now, the sun will not shine," said the second one.

"I agree more with you than with the first forecast," said the third meteorologist.

Why was the third meteorologist so sure?

172

A criminal took his wife to the movies to watch a western. During a gunshot scene he killed his wife with a bullet to her heart. When he left the movies with his wife's dead body, nobody tried to stop him. How did he manage this?

173

In the fifth century A.D. a king was taking his daily bath when he received a huge crown that he had ordered made from one of his bars of gold. He knew that the crown and the gold weighed the same, although he suspected that part of the gold had been replaced with lighter materials, such as copper or silver. How did he find out quickly?

174

If I take two apples out of a basket containing six apples, how many apples do I have?

175

How much will a 38-degree angle measure when observed under a microscope that magnifies ten times?

36

176

John Peterson was born in Albany in 1938, on a date not divisible by 2, 3, or 5, and in a month that does not contain the letter "e" or "i". When does he become one year older?

177

A passenger traveling by bus between Springfield and Capital City noticed that due to the heavy traffic, it took him 80 minutes to reach his destination at an average speed of 40 mph. On his return trip, he took the bus and it took him 1 hour and 20 minutes at the same average speed and with less traffic. Do you know why?

178

A man traveling in a taxi is talking to the driver. After a while, the driver tells him, "You must excuse me, but I am deaf and cannot hear a word of what you are saying." The passenger stops talking. After he gets out of the cab, the passenger realizes that the driver had lied to him. How?

179

A friend told me the following story: "I was drinking a Coke in a bar when a man wearing a mustache came in and ordered a glass of water. As the waiter came back with his water, he pointed a gun at the customer. The customer got startled, but then calmed down and thanked the waiter." How can you explain what happened?

180

A 30-year-old man married a 25-year-old woman. She died at the age of 50 and her husband was so devastated that he cried for years. Ten years after he stopped crying, he died. However, he lived to be 80. How many years was he a widower?

181

Two rich men, now bankrupt, came across each other one day. After exchanging greetings and catching up with what had happened in their lives, they compared how much money each had. The first one had $80 and the second one had only $42. However, two hours later, between both of them they had more than $84 million in cash. Neither of them had inherited anything, won the lottery, or received payment for a debt or loan. How could this be?

182

I am sitting at a table. Ten flies are on the table. With one swat, I kill three flies. How many flies are left on the table?

INTELLIGENCE AND SKILLS

183

How can you drop a matchbook match from five feet above the ground so that it comes to rest with one of its thin edges touching the ground?

184

How can you drop an egg a distance of three feet without breaking it?

185

How can you divide a round pie in eight equal pieces by cutting only three straight lines?

186

Two thin ropes hang from the high ceiling of an empty room, just too far apart from each other to be grabbed with both hands at the same time. How can you tie a knot with both rope ends using only a pair of sharp scissors?

187

A sparrow has fallen into a hole in a rock. The hole measures three inches in diameter and is three feet deep. Due to the depth of the hole, the sparrow cannot be reached by hand. We cannot use sticks or canes, because we could hurt the bird. How can you get the bird out?

188

A homeless man runs out of cigarettes. He looks for cigarette butts since he knows that he can make one new cigarette out of every three butts. He picks up nine butts. If he smokes one cigarette per hour, how many hours can he smoke for?

189

How can you make a hole in a paper napkin and then fit your body through it without tearing the napkin?

190

How can you form four equilateral triangles with six toothpicks of equal length?

191

You go on a picnic with your friends. Each one of them wants a different amount of oil and vinegar in his salad. However, you've already mixed the oil and vinegar in one bottle. How can you please everyone at the picnic?

192

The maximum length of a postal package is 30 inches. How can you mail an iron bar that measures 40 inches in length without bending it?

193

How can you tie a knot with a napkin by holding one end in each hand without letting go of it?

194

If you cut a circle the size of a nickel in a piece of paper, can you pass a silver dollar through it?

195

A six-foot-long rope is tied to a hook fixed to the ceiling of a room. We tie a mug by the handle to the loose end of the rope. If you cut the rope in half, how can you prevent the mug from falling? (There is nothing between the floor and the mug. Nobody is holding on to the mug.)

196

Two thick ropes hang from a high ceiling attached to hooks three feet apart. The ends touch the ground. Without using anything else, and considering that you will die if you fall from one-quarter of the height of the room, how can you cut the largest amount possible of each rope with a knife?

197

You are playing table tennis on the beach when your only ball falls into a hole in the sand that someone else had used for their beach umbrella. The hole is only slightly larger in diameter than the ball. How can you take the ball out without digging?

198

A truck is about to go under a bridge, although its load is two inches higher than the clearance of the bridge. It is a very heavy load, so it cannot be unloaded. How can it pass under the bridge in a quick and simple way?

199

How could you throw a tennis ball so that after traveling a short distance, it stops and returns following the same path? The ball cannot hit or be tied to anything.

200

A brick measuring 5 centimeters high, 20 centimeters long, and 10 centimeters wide falls off a dike, causing a leak that must be stopped immediately. How can you stop the leak with a saw and a wooden cylinder measuring 5 centimeters in diameter?

201

With your pants on, can you put your right hand in your left pocket and your left hand in your right pocket?

202

I bet that you alone cannot take off your left shoe using only your right hand. I will not touch you or interfere with your movements. How can I prevent this?

203

How can you pour wine out of a corked bottle that is half full without breaking or damaging the bottle or the cork, and without taking out the cork?

204

You keep some of your diamonds in a jewelry case with a sliding cover. To keep thieves away, you put a scorpion inside the case. One day you need to take some of the diamonds. How can you do it without taking the scorpion out, while protecting your hands from its bites, only taking a few seconds, and leaving the case in the same way you originally had it?

205

I am going to make you a bet: "On this folded piece of paper I have written down the prediction of something that might or might not happen in the next five minutes. Put it in your pocket. On this blank piece of paper, write "YES" if you think that it will happen and "NO" if you think it will not happen. I'll bet you a cup of coffee that you cannot guess right." What have I written on the paper? (It is something that can be proven.)

206

Your rich relative gathers the family together to tell them, "I will leave my inheritance to the one who can collect the exact number of pennies equaling half the number of days that I have left to live." What would you do to inherit the fortune?

207

How can two people step on one page of newspaper so that they can't touch each other without stepping off the newspaper?

208

A friend told me, "I can do something that you are not able to, no matter how hard you try." What could it be?

209

A bottle is standing on a rug (or upside down on a dollar bill). Can you take out the rug or the bill without turning or touching the bottle and without help from anybody else?

210

Set an imaginary finish line somewhere (for example, a point on the wall ten feet away from you). Find a method of advancing so that even though you always move ahead, you never reach the finish line.

211

Yesterday, someone dared me to jump over a ballpoint pen on the floor. I could not, even though I'm a good jumper. How come I wasn't able to?

INVESTIGATIONS AND TRIALS

212

A plane was hijacked. The hijacker demanded two parachutes and ten million dollars. Once he got both, he jumped off the plane during the night and while in flight. Why did he need two parachutes?

213

One rainy day, my cousin Ernest found a dead body lying next to a strange package. He could not see any footprints in the area. Because of the temperature of the body, Ernest knew that the man had been dead for less than one hour. What was in the package? How did the man get there?

214

A man walking along a rural road was being sought by the police. When he saw a patrol car approaching him, he thought of running toward the forest. Instead, he ran 20 yards toward the approaching car. Why?

215

Stella was telling my cousin Ernest that her husband once fell asleep in the opera and started dreaming of being on a plane that was hijacked. The hijacker demanded to fly to an African country. People complained, screamed, and fainted. The hijacker was pointing a gun to Stella's husband's head. At this point, the husband started to move and make noise. Stella tapped her husband on the shoulder and he got so startled that he fell on the floor and died from the impact. Ernest immediately said, "This story is impossible." How did he know?

216

My cousin Ernest solved this case. A man was hanged, his feet half a meter above the ground, in the middle of a very hot room, hanging by a rope tied to a hook from the ceiling. The room was completely empty and had some moisture on the floor. On the other side of the door there was a ladder, which must have been used by the victim. However, the investigation proved that the victim had no place to lean the ladder against to reach the rope. That is how Ernest realized that this was not a murder, but a suicide. How could it have happened?

217

Last winter, my cousin Ernest went on a ski vacation. At the airport, he read in the papers that a famous couple had been skiing and the wife had died in an accident. Her well-known husband was the only eyewitness. After talking to a travel agent, my cousin was able to deduce that it had not been an accident. What did he find out from the travel agent?

218

A medieval count organized a court trial in which he gave the defendant a chance to save his life if he could pick a white marble out of a bag containing, in the count's words, one white marble and one black marble. The accused knew that this was a trick, because he had seen the count place two black marbles in the bag. However, he went ahead and took out a marble. What did he do to save his life?

219

During the war, my cousin Ernest was captured and put into a prison cell. It was in the basement, with a dirt floor, armored walls, and a water tank ten feet from the ground. There was no furniture and no object to reach the water tank with. How did Ernest manage to drink?

220

My cousin Ernest, amateur private investigator, was able to figure out the weapon used in a suicide case. The man had been stabbed, but the weapon was nowhere in the room. The room was locked from the inside. The deceased had the only key. During the investigation, they found out that the weapon had been thicker than typical knives. What was the weapon? Where was it?

221

When Ernest went to visit his friend Albert, he found him dead on his desk with a bullet through the head. He saw a cassette player and decided to listen to the tape. He hit "play" and heard, "This is Albert. I just got a call saying that someone is on his way here to kill me and that he will be here in less than three minutes. I hear steps. Someone is opening the door." At that point, my cousin knew that it was not Albert's voice on the tape, but the killer's. How did he know that?

222

A man has been killed in a room locked from the inside with a vertical deadbolt. The killer was able to lock it from the outside.
How did he do this?

223

A businessman was working in his home office when he realized he had left a five-dollar bill in the book he had been reading. He called his butler to bring him the book from the library. When he got the book, the bill was no longer there. He then questioned the maid and the butler. The maid remembered seeing the bill between pages 99 and 100 in a book to the left of a business book. The butler did not recall seeing the bill, but was sure the book was to the right of the business book, because to the left of it there was a statistics book. Who is lying?

224

On the 29th of last month, there was a double murder on the express train from Paris to Berlin. The engineer and the conductor were killed at the same time, even though they were at opposite ends of the train. This was confirmed by a police detective, who was at the exact center of the train and heard both gunshots at the same time.

When my cousin was told this story, he realized that both victims did not die at the same time.

How did he figure it out?

225

Two people were accused of murder. In a court trial, one had been acquitted and the other had been found guilty. When the judge had to sentence the guilty man, he said, "This is the strangest case that I have ever presided over. Even though you have been found guilty, the law obliges me to set you free." Can you explain this?

226

My cousin Ernest was once kidnapped. He knew they would either take him to New York City or to Sydney, Australia. When they took his blindfold off, he could see he had been locked in a room without windows. There was only a table, a bed, a chair, and a sink. However, Ernest was able to figure out which city he was in. How did he do it?

227

These are the clues to a robbery and murder in a ground floor office:

A. The killer had to be one of these three people: the muscled engineer, the obese director, or the perky secretary.

B. The stolen goods were taken out from the open window. There were light footprints under it in the snow.

C. The footprints matched the director's shoes, which were found next to the crime weapon.

D. Only one bullet was found, although there were two wounds to the body, one to the chest and the other to the right hand.

Who was the killer? Why were there two wounds?

RIDDLES

228

I climbed up a cherry tree, where I found cherries. I did not pick cherries, nor did I leave cherries. How can you explain this?

229

What animal walks on all fours in the morning, on two legs at noon, and on three legs at dusk?

230

What is so fragile that when you say its name you break it?

231

Among my siblings I am the thinnest. I am in Paris, but I am not in France. Who am I?

232

I can only live when there is light, although I die if the light shines on me. What am I?

ELEMENTS IN MOVEMENT

233

A ship is anchored offshore. In order for the crew to reach the rafts, they must descend a 22-step ladder. Each step is ten inches high. The tide rises at a ratio of five inches per hour. How many steps will the tide have covered after ten hours?

234

A 100-meter-long train moving 100 meters per minute must pass through a tunnel of 100 meters in length. How long will it take?

235

A train headed for Barcelona leaves Madrid at midnight, at a constant speed of 60 kilometers per hour. Another train leaves Barcelona at the same time, heading for Madrid at a constant speed of 40 kilometers per hour. The distance between both cities is 600 kilometers. The train that left from Madrid stops for half an hour when both trains cross. Which train was closer to Madrid when they crossed?

236

My uncle Lou takes the subway to the movies or the theater every evening. He always takes the first subway that stops at the station close to his home, no matter which direction it is heading. If the subway is heading north, he will go to the theater. If it is heading south, he will go to the movies. Both trains run every ten minutes. However, nine times out of every ten, my uncle ends up at the movies. How can you explain this?

237

A cyclist takes 2 minutes and 13 seconds for every full lap of a circuit. Answer in 10 seconds: How long will he take to do 60 laps?

238

My bird can fly faster than any supersonic plane. How can this be?

239

Albert, who was just back from his trip around the world in a sailboat, asked me, "What part of my boat has traveled the longest distance?" Do you know the answer to that?

240

If we tie a light oxygen tank to a bird so that it can breathe on the moon, would the bird fly faster, slower, or the same speed as it does on earth? (Remember that there is less gravity on the moon.)

241

What can a train passenger do to be in a tunnel the least time possible while the train is going through a 100-meter-long tunnel?

242

Two trains travel on parallel tracks in opposite directions, at 70 and 50 miles per hour. When the trains are 60 miles apart, a bird flying at 80 miles per hour leaves the first train and flies off to the second. It keeps on flying back and forth until both trains cross. How many miles does the bird fly?

243

We drag a large stone over three logs measuring 50 inches in circumference each. What distance does the stone cover each time the logs make one rotation?

244

Two trains are moving on the same track in opposite directions. One goes 80 meters per minute and the other 120 meters per minute. After 12 hours, they are 1,700 meters apart. How far apart will they be one minute before they collide?

245

A snail is climbing up a one-meter-high wall. It advances three centimeters per minute and then stops for one minute to rest, during which it slides back down two centimeters. How long will the snail take to reach the top of the wall?

246

A young man gets on the end car of a train. Just as the train passes by Cat City, he leaves his suitcases and walks at a steady pace to find a seat. After five minutes, he reaches the front car. Not finding a seat, he returns at the same pace to where his luggage is. At that point, the train passes by Dog City, which is five miles from Cat City. How fast is the train going?

247

A journey by ship between New York and London takes seven days. Ships leave from both ports at the same time every day. During the trip, how many other ships will a ship come across?

248

A regular LP record measures 30 centimeters in diameter. The outer blank (non-recorded) area is 5 millimeters in width. The non-playable center area measures 10 centimeters in diameter. The grooves are ¼ millimeter apart. What is the distance traveled by the needle during the time that the record is playing?

249

A man is walking at night at a steady pace. As he passes by a street lamp, he notices that his shadow becomes longer. Does the top of the shadow move faster, slower, or the same when the shadow is longer as when it is shorter?

250

A kid who is in the back seat of a car is holding the string of a helium balloon. The balloon is floating without touching the roof of the car, and the windows are closed. When the car accelerates, where does the balloon go? And when the car turns, where does it go?

251

A train goes from north to south, although at all times there are certain areas of the train that are moving in a south-to-north direction. What are these areas?

252

A railway track measures five kilometers in length and its ties are one meter apart. A child ties a can to a dog's tail. As the dog starts running along the tracks, it increases its speed by one meter per second every time it hears the noise of the can hitting a tie. If the dog starts to run at a speed of one meter per second and the can hits all of the railway ties, what is the dog's speed at the end of the track?

253

Two athletes ran in a 100-meter race. When the runner with the number "1" on his jersey reached the finish line, the runner with number "2" had only run 95 meters. In a second race, the number "1" runner had to start 5 meters behind the start line. If both ran at the same speed as in the first race, who won this time?

254

A driver always leaves the office at the same time, gets to the director's house at the same time, picks him up, and takes him to the office. One morning, the director decides to leave one hour earlier and he starts walking to the office along his usual route. When he sees the car, he gets in and continues his trip. He reaches the office 20 minutes earlier than usual. How long was he walking for?

255

In a river without a current, a ship leaves from a certain point, goes three miles up the river, turns around, and goes back to the point of departure in 20 minutes. If the river has a current of two miles per hour and the ship did the same trip at the same speed (with respect to the water), would the trip last more or less than 20 minutes?

256

A mountaineer starts rapidly climbing up a mountain trail at 6 a.m. He makes frequent and irregular stops to rest or eat. He reaches the summit at 6 p.m. At 6 a.m. the next day, he starts his way back following the same route, stopping only once to eat. He reaches the starting point at 6 p.m. Is there a point on the way where he passes at exactly the same time on both days?

OUTDOORS

257

Which is warmer, a two-inch-thick blanket or two blankets one-inch-thick each?

258

Three ice cubes are melting in a glass of water. Once they have completely melted, has the water level of the glass changed?

259

A super-accurate bomb, one that always hits the bull's-eye and destroys it, hits an indestructible fort. What will happen?

260

A man gets up 180 times every night and sleeps for at least seven hours at a stretch. Where does he live?

261

I had just made myself a cup of coffee when I realized I had to run upstairs for a moment. I did not want the coffee to get cold, and I had to add milk at room temperature. Should I add the milk before I go up or after I get back?

262

A raft loaded with rocks is floating in a swimming pool. We mark the level of water in the swimming pool and on the raft. If we drop the rocks into the pool, what will happen to the water level in the pool and to the flotation line of the raft? Will they go up or down?

263

A boat is floating in a pool. We mark the flotation line. If we drop rocks into the pool and make the water level rise five inches, will the water rise more or less than five inches compared to the mark we made on the boat?

264

Two ivy branches sprout out of a tree trunk from the same point at ground level. One wraps around four times to the right, the other wraps around five times to the left, and their ends meet. Without counting the ends, how many times do both branches of ivy intersect?

265

An African trader is visiting different tribes in a raft loaded with sacks of salt, which he trades according to their weight in gold. When he is about to trade them, he realizes that the scale is broken. How can he trade the same weight of salt for gold?

A LITTLE BIT OF EVERYTHING

266

We have a bottle of wine approximately three fourths full. We want to leave an amount of wine in the bottle equal to exactly half of the total capacity of the bottle. How can we do it without using anything to help us?

267

We have three glass pitchers. One is a three-quart pitcher and is empty. The twelve-quart one is also empty. The third one is clear in color and irregular in shape. It contains acid. It has two marks, a two-quart mark and a five-quart mark. The level of acid is a little less than five quarts. We want to take out exactly three quarts of acid, but when we try it, the three-quart pitcher breaks. What can we do to take out the desired amount by pouring it into the twelve-quart pitcher, which is the only one left?

268

A man was used to walking at a regular pace. He never wore a watch, although he had a very accurate clock at home. One day, he forgot to wind it and the clock stopped. He went to a friend's house two miles from his home to ask the time. He spent the afternoon with him and when he came back home, he set the clock to the exact time. How did he know the exact time?

269

We have two similar coins and we make one spin on the edge of the other. How many times does the spinning coin turn on itself each time it takes an entire lap around the stationary one?

270

Mr. Brown, Mr. White, and Mr. Red are in a meeting. The three are wearing ties that are the three colors of their last names, although no man's tie matches his name. Mr. Brown asks the man with the white tie if he likes red, but cannot hear the answer. What is the color of each man's tie?

271

We mark three random points on a sphere. How likely are the three points to be in the same hemisphere?

272

Can you draw a square with two straight lines?

LAUGHS

273

My cousin Henry can predict the future when he pets his black poodle. Is that possible?

274

An older woman and her young daughter, a young man, and an older man are traveling in the same compartment of a train. When the train passes through a tunnel, they hear a kiss and a slap. As the lights come back on, they can see the older man with a black eye. This is what each of the passengers thought:

The older woman: "He deserved it. I am glad my daughter can defend herself."

The daughter: "I cannot believe he preferred to kiss my mother or that young man over kissing me."

The older man: "What is going on here? I didn't do anything! Maybe the young man tried to kiss the girl, and she mistakenly slapped me."

The young man: "I know what really happened."

Do you know what happened?

275

An electric train runs at 60 mph heading south toward a wind blowing at 30 mph. What is the direction of the smoke from the train?

276

If Albert's peacock jumps over the fence onto Edward's property and lays an egg there, whose egg is it?

277

What can you have in an empty pocket? (Apart from air, of course.)

278

What did the twelve apostles make?

279

My cousin Herbert told me yesterday, "I can easily bite my eye." How can this be?

280

It sings and has ten feet. What is it?

281

Mary married John two years ago. She did not bring any money into the marriage and did not work during these two years, but she made her husband a millionaire. How did she do it?

282

My cousin Herbert told me this morning, "I can easily bite my good eye." How can he do this?

283

What can elephants make that no other animal can?

284

Last Thursday I walked back home from work (two miles), and noticed a strange man following me the entire way. Once I got home, the man was still there walking around my building (a 100-by-100-yard-square building). Later on, I saw he had fallen asleep next to the street lamp at the entrance of my building. During which lap did he fall asleep?

285

How can you get into your home if there is a dangerous dog inside that doesn't know you and belongs to your wife's friend?

286

A turtle, a gopher, and a hare are walking one behind the other in a straight line.

"I am first," said the turtle.

"I am second," said the gopher.

"I am first," said the hare.

How can you explain these statements?

287

What activity can only be done at night?

288

My cousin Robert was pushed into a well measuring six feet in diameter and ten feet deep, with smooth walls and its bottom covered with water. How did he emerge from the well?

289

Every day, a cyclist crosses the border between Spain and France carrying a bag. No matter how much customs officials investigate him, they do not know what he is smuggling. Do you?

Answers

1. Only once, because the second time you will be subtracting from 24 instead of 30.

2. The number 8. (It is made up of two zeroes, one on top of the other.)

3. By using Roman numerals. The upper half of XII is VII.

4. 1 and 9.

5. Any number and 1.

6. 2 and 2.

7. It is easy to eliminate possibilities. For example, it has to be an even number; none of the digits can be 0 (or else the product would be 0); and the product of the digits must be less than or equal to 48 (otherwise two times the product would have three digits). If you think of the remaining possibilities, you will find the answer, $36 = 2 \times 3 \times 6$.

8. 1, 2, and 3, because $1 \times 2 \times 3 = 1 + 2 + 3 = 6$.

9. $25 = 5^2$ and $36 = 6^2$.

10. $9^{9^9} = 9^{387420489}$, which is a number with more than 369 million digits.

11. The father is 41 and the son is 14.

12. 10¢.

13. $1.10 for the outlet and $0.10 for the lightbulb.

14. $3 \times 75 = 225$ qualities distributed among 100 persons, so at least 25% of them have all three.

15. The number of passing grades is a whole number less than 32, and 5% of it is also a whole number. It can only be 20. If 20 is the number of passing grades, the number of students from New York that took the test is one.

16. If half of the 83% tip the usher 10¢ and the other half doesn't, it is the same as if all 83% had tipped him 5¢, which is the same amount as what the remaining 17% tipped. The usher received 4,800¢, or more simply, $48.

17. Turn the page upside down. It will read 108 = 6 x 18.

18. He will need twenty "9's," one for the numbers 9, 19, 29, 39, 49, 59, 69, 79, 89, 90, 91, 92, 93, 94, 95, 96, 97, and 98, and two for 99.

19. At each stop, passengers can buy a ticket for any of the 24 remaining stops. Therefore, the number of tickets will be 25 x 24 = 600.

20. Let's imagine that the inhabitants are as different as possible (one will be bald, another will have only one hair, another two, another three, and so on, until we get to someone having 100,000 hairs). Inhabitant number 100,002 will have the same number of hairs as someone among the first 100,001 inhabitants. The total population is more than 200,000 people, which means that there will be more than 100,000 inhabitants with the same number of hairs as other people in town.

21. Three: one red, one blue, and one brown.

22. There are six chestnut trees per side, making a total of 12.

23. Two birds and one olive tree.

24. There is only one winner, so the remaining 110 players were defeated in 110 matches. Therefore, they used 110 balls.

25. Twelve muffins. When John ate half the remaining muffins plus three more to leave none, he must have eaten six muffins. So Peter ate half the muffins and left six, meaning that there were 12 to start.

26. The shepherd that is talking has five sheep and the other one has seven.

27. Three cages and four canaries.

28. Each sardine costs 1 dollar. Therefore, 7½ sardines would cost 7½ dollars.

29. Since ½ brick weighs 3 pounds, 1½ bricks weigh 9 pounds.

30. Since 18 sardines is the same as 1½ dozen, they cost 9 ½ dollars.

31. Since 1 man eats 1 pie in 1½ minutes, 1 man eats 20 pies in 30 minutes, which means 3 men eat 60 pies in 30 minutes.

32. 11 times (one fewer than the number of times he went in).

33. Three ducks.

34. The person who won three games must have also lost six games, since his opponent won $3. In total, they played nine games.

35. We measure the inside diameter and the height of the liquid, obtaining the volume of the liquid. Then, we turn the bottle upside down and measure the volume of the empty part. If we add both, we obtain the total capacity of the bottle and can calculate the percentage of the liquid. An easier way is to measure only both heights, because both have the same size base.

36. $0.0125.

37. By leaving a task half done (for example, peeling potatoes) so that the next soldier can finish it, they can do all the tasks in 1 hour and 30 minutes.

38. 29 days. One spider would have covered half of the space on the 29th day, and on the 30th day would repeat what had been done, covering the space completely. Two spiders would each have covered half of the space in 29 days, therefore covering the entire area.

39. At 8 p.m. Each hour the volume triples, so it is one-third full one hour before it is full.

40. If the length of the rope + 2 yards = 3 times the length of the rope, then the rope is 1 yard long.

41. If the length is 6 yards + half the length, then half the length is 6 yards. Therefore, it is 12 yards long.

42. No mud at all, because a hole can only contain air.

43. There are only three people, a daughter, her mother, and her grandmother. The mother received 25 books from the grandmother and then gave 8 to her daughter.

44. Dolores is taller than Emily, who is taller than Ann.

45. Joan is six years older than Rose.

46. Emily speaks in a softer voice than Dolores

    (Emily < Ann < Dolores).

47. Peter is sitting between Philip (on his right) and James (on his left).

48. A pound of $10 gold coins has twice the amount of gold as half a pound of $20 coins. Therefore, it is worth more.

49. The store lost $40 given as change plus the value of the umbrella, $10. The transaction was only between the salesperson and the customer. The bank teller did not take part in the transaction.

50. The pitcher with water contains exactly the same amount of wine as water in the pitcher of wine. Both pitchers have the same volume of liquid before and after mixing water and wine, so mixing them makes no difference.

51. He made each candidate ride another candidate's horse. Each one would, of course, try to come in first, because in that way the owner of the horse that a particular candidate was riding would lose the race.

52. The weight of the fishbowl increases by the same amount as the weight of the liquid displaced by the fish.

53. If it is a traditional scale with two dishes, you can place the apples in one dish and dirt in the other until they balance. Then, replace the apples with weights and you will know the weight of the apples. If it is a spring scale, you weigh the apples first, then write down the mark on the scale and replace the apples with weights until you reach the previous mark. The weights will show the real weight of the apples.

54. The reaction of the air that the little bird is pushing down in order to fly will partially affect both the dish of the scale and the floor of the room. The scale will show one pound minus some portion of the five ounces that the bird weighs. If the cage were sealed, the air would affect only the dish of the scale and the scale would continue to read one pound.

55. One weighing. Take one ball from the first sack, two from the second, three from the third, and so on until you reach the last sack, from which you take ten balls. Since $1 + 2 + 3 + ... + 9 + 10 = 55$, if all of the balls weighed 10 ounces each, the total weight would be 550 ounces. In this case the weight will be $550 - N$, where N is the number of the sack containing nine-ounce balls.

56. We identify each sack by the number of balls taken from it. We must find a way to obtain different results from all possible sums of the digits that identify the sacks. The easiest way would be powers of 2: 1, 2, 4, 8, 16, ... (2^0, 2^1, 2^2, 2^3, 2^4, ...). Therefore, we will take one ball from one sack, two from another, four from another, etc.

The resulting weight will be $1023 - N$, where N can only be obtained by adding certain sack numbers. If N is 27 ounces, the sacks containing 9-ounce balls will be those from which we took 1, 2, 8, and 16 balls, because, using just the powers of 2, 27 can only be obtained by adding $1 + 2 + 8 + 16$.

Let's call "1" the sack from which we took 1 ball, "2" the one from which we took 2 balls, "3" the one from which we took 4 balls, etc. The number 27, in binary, is 11011. The position of the 1's in this binary sequence reveals the solution. The 1's are in first, second, fourth, and fifth position, which means that the sacks containing the 9-ounce balls are 1, 2, 4, and 5.

57. The best solution is to open four links from one of the pieces and use them to join the remaining five parts in one chain. The total cost will be $4 \times 60 = 240$¢, or \$2.40.

58. By cutting the third link, we obtain three pieces of one, two, and four links each. The first day, she pays with the one-link part. The second day, she pays with the two-link part and gets the one-link part back as change. The third day, she pays with the loose link. The fourth day, she pays with the four-link part and receives back the three links, and so on.

59. The minimum number of parts that could have been left is three (the link that is cut and the two disconnected parts of the chain). The maximum number will be six, as shown in the figure below.

60. Two glasses. Pick up the second glass, pour its contents into the ninth glass, and put it back. Then pick up the fourth glass, pour its contents into the seventh glass, and put it back. Note that the seventh and ninth glasses are not moved.

61. 100% probability, because if four marbles are in their corresponding cups, the fifth one must be in its corresponding cup, too.

62. Three. The first two can be of different colors, white and black, but the third sock will be one of these two colors, and thus complete one pair.

63. Four. There are three different colors, so the first three socks may not match, but the fourth one will match one of the previous three socks.

64. 13. The first 12 gloves can be six white left gloves and six black left gloves. Therefore, the 13th glove will make a pair with one of the previous 12 gloves. No matter what the first 12 gloves are, if no two have made a pair yet, the 13th will.

65. Six. The worst case is to take two white, two black, and the red marble. The sixth marble has to be either white or black.

66. Put five marbles in one cup, four in another and one in another. Put the cup with one marble inside the one containing four. There are other solutions, all based on the same trick. Another solution, for example, involves putting three marbles in one cup, three marbles in the second cup, and four marbles in the third cup, and then putting the second cup inside the third one. This leaves three marbles in the first cup, three marbles in the second cup, and seven marbles in the third cup.

67. Put one marble in one box, three in another box, and five in a third one. Then place the three boxes inside the fourth box.

68. Take one marble from the box marked BW. If it is white, the other marble must also be white. This means that the box marked BB must have black and white marbles and the box marked WW must have only black marbles. You can apply the same principle if the first marble you take is black.

69. After being inverted twice, the hourglass continued working in its initial position. Therefore, the extra hour that it measured was a consequence of these two inversions, half an hour each time. If it was inverted for the second time at 11:30 a.m., the first time had to be a half-hour earlier, at 11:00 a.m.

70. The clock that doesn't work will show the precise time twice a day, but the fast one will take 2 x 60 x 12 = 1440 days to show the precise time. Therefore, the broken clock shows the correct time more often.

71. Time to have the clock fixed.

72. Ten times (you can verify it yourself).

73. Four seconds (it takes two seconds between two consecutive strikes).

74. Four hours, the time between eight o'clock and twelve o'clock.

75. There is one second between two strikes. Therefore, it will take 11 seconds for the clock to strike 12 times.

76. He lived 59 years, because there is no "0" year.

77. He would have drunk the same number of cups of coffee. The difference is that the conversation would have taken place on March 14.

78. Friday.

79. Three days and two nights. She left yesterday and will return tomorrow.

80. The man's birthday is December 31 and he was talking on January 1. He is 36 now, the day before yesterday he was 35, this calendar year he will turn 37, and next calendar year he will turn 38.

81. It happened to Gioacchino Rossini, who was born on February 29, 1792, and who died on November 13, 1868. Remember that 1800 was not a leap year. All years that are divisible by four are leap years, except those that end in "00". They are only leap years if they are divisible by 400.

82. Invent.

83. Neither. The yolk of an egg is yellow.

84. It is not "I AM GOING IN" or "I AM NOT GOING IN". The opposite is "I AM LEAVING".

85. The word "incorrectly."

86. Lounger.

87. It's a matter of language. Consider "four twenty" as $4.20. Then it is true.

88. Yes. "Paris" starts with a "p", and "ends" starts with an "e".

89. The phone operator was trying to get the spelling of the man's last name. Therefore, it makes no sense to ask, "I as in what"? The operator had already understood it was an "I".

90. The letter "i".

91. Let's suppose it is false. By saying "This statement is false," it becomes true and vice versa. Therefore, to be false it has to be true and vice versa. It is a paradox.

92. The letter "u".

93. He will not change his mind.

94. His statement must be "I will be hanged." If they want to hang him, the sentence is true, and therefore, they will not be able to hang him. For the same reason, he cannot be drowned because his statement would be false and they could not drown him if his statement is false. (Based on **Don Quixote,** by Cervantes.)

95. Yes, as long as the other half are male, too. She has five sons.

96. Nine children.

97. Three more brothers than sisters. Ann's brother has one more brother than sister. Ann is one of the sisters, so Ann will have one fewer sister than her brother has and one more brother than her brother has.

98. Seven. The only possible solution is that the person talking is a woman and there are four women and three men.

99. The doctor is a woman.

100. John is Raymond's son.

101. Your mother.

102. The son's mother.

103. The second man is Charles's grandson.

104. No, because it would be his mother.

105. The man is Ann's uncle.

106. If the man left a widow, then he is dead. Therefore, he cannot get married.

107. She was looking at a photo of her nephew.

108. He was looking at a photo of his father.

109. Two widowers have one daughter each and decide to marry each other's daughters. This conversation takes place once they are married and with children. Their wives are the ones talking.

110. The Pacific Ocean. Even though it had not been discovered or named by Balboa, it was still the biggest ocean.

111. One cookie, because after eating one you would no longer have an empty stomach.

112. Because it wasn't raining.

113. Holes.

114. By walking and dragging the rope with it. The puzzle does not say that the leash is tied to something.

115. The number "400" to hang on a house. This number is formed by three digits, at $1 each.

116. It was daytime, so the room was light.

117. With one quarter and one nickel. The puzzle says that one of the coins is not a nickel, and it is true since a quarter is not a nickel.

118. Because he earns double by giving a haircut to two foreigners instead of to only one person in town.

119. He goes to the next room and by crawling toward the bottle, he slides into the room.

120. The plane had not yet taken off.

121. He had already put sugar in his coffee.

122. The match.

123. By serving mashed potatoes.

124. It is a male giraffe, so it is the father and not the mother of the offspring.

125. Ten cows. We can call the pigs cows, but it doesn't make them cows.

126. He must always be behind the whistle.

127. There is no reason to baptize him. If he is Catholic, he is already baptized.

128. The letter "e".

129. My uncle Emil is blind, and he was reading in Braille.

130. He is a farmer. He needs plenty of water, so if he lacks water he has no income and he won't be able to buy or even make wine.

131. At the beginning of the puzzle, it says that you are the cab driver. Therefore, the answer is your name and age.

132. One of the trains went into the tunnel hours after the other.

133. It was a girls' team.

134. My aunt Martha was a pedestrian, too.

135. The customers paid $27, $25 to cover their bill, and $2 as a tip for the waiter.

136. The driver of the moped was the policeman's son.

137. The butcher's daughter is the fisherman's wife.

138. Since he's a butcher, he weighs meat.

139. The first four people pick one apple each, and the fifth one takes the basket with the apple in it.

140. Either a deep-sea diver or an astronaut.

141. "To sint" means to take off your clothes, and "to sant" is to go into the water to bathe.

142. Because before the game begins, the score is always 0 – 0.

143. I deposited $50 in my bank account to have enough funds to cash the check.

144. The passenger gave the driver 25¢ in the form of four nickels and five pennies.

145. Nine.

146. As far as half of the forest, because if she went any further, she would be leaving the forest, instead of going into it.

147. All the animals that have one, because as far as we know, no animal takes it off to eat.

148. You just have to light a match under a container with water.

149. Straight, arced, or spiral.

150. The parrot was deaf.

151. The surgeon was the boy's mother.

152. Because there are fewer black sheep than white sheep.

153. She dropped her earring into her coffee beans.

154. The dictionary. The work "foreword" comes before "epilogue," "end" is in the first half of the dictionary, and "index" comes before "introduction".

155. The girl's name is Anne COUPLE.

156. If it were an authentic coin, it could not have the letters "B.C." (This system was created after Jesus died, not before he was born.)

157. Neither country, because they are survivors.

158. What the director actually needed was a real night-shift guard that did not sleep at work, even if he could predict the future in his dreams.

159. My cousin Edward is bald. Therefore, his hair cannot get wet.

160. My aunt is really short and the button for the 25th floor is at the highest point she can reach.

161. The neighbor was snoring. That is why he couldn't sleep. When he made the call, the person woke up and stopped snoring.

162. He must turn on both faucets at the same time.

163. The woman died before the operation.

164. If three of the letters are correct, the fourth one must be too. Therefore, there is only one way.

165. The same month you are reading this.

166. The river was frozen.

167. When he sees his coworker, the miner with the clean face assumes that his face is also dirty and wipes it. The miner with a dirty face sees his coworker with a clean face and assumes that his is also clean.

168. The letter "g".

169. Hairdressers don't cut their own hair. Therefore, the clean hairdresser gave the bad haircut and the dirty hairdresser gave the perfect haircut. Thus, it is better to go to the dirty salon.

170. The customer was in his firefighter uniform.

171. Because in 96 hours it would again be night.

172. It was a drive-in theater. He killed her in the car. On his way out, nobody noticed that the woman was dead in the car.

173. First he immersed the crown in a container of water and measured the level of the water. Then he removed the crown and immersed the gold bar, measuring the water level. If the levels were not the same, the gold had been mixed with another metal.

174. Two apples.

175. It will still be 38 degrees.

176. On his birthday.

177. He took the same time in both cases, because 1 hour and 20 minutes equals 80 minutes.

178. If the cab driver had been deaf, he would not have heard the address the passenger had given him. He only mentioned he was deaf when the passenger didn't stop talking.

179. The waiter scared his customer who had the hiccups. That is why the customer thanked the waiter.

180. If he became a widower when he was 55 and died when he was 80, he was a widower for 25 years.

181. One was standing at the main door of a bank and his friend was standing at the back door. There was $84 million in the safe of the bank. Therefore, "between both of them" they had that amount of money.

182. I killed three flies. They remain. The rest would have flown away immediately.

183. By bending the match and then dropping it.

184. Drop it and catch it before it hits the ground.

185. Cutting it either of these ways.

186. Tie the scissors to one of the ropes and make it move like a pendulum. Then take the other end of the rope and grab the scissors as they come toward you. Then tie the knot.

187. By gradually pouring sand into the hole. The bird will keep moving so that it is not buried in the sand, forcing it higher until it comes out.

188. He makes three cigarettes out of the nine cigarette butts. Every time he smokes one cigarette, he has one new cigarette butt. In total, he smokes four cigarettes and, therefore, smokes for four hours.

189. Cut it either of these ways:

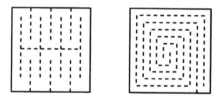

190. In two dimensions there is no solution, but it is possible in three dimensions, where you can form a tetrahedron.

191. Oil floats in vinegar. All you have to do is to tilt the bottle. To pour vinegar, you have to turn the bottle upside down, and by pulling off the cork a little, you can let the desired amount of vinegar out.

192. By placing it diagonally in a 30-by-30-inch package.

193. Cross your arms and hold a tip of the napkin in each hand. When you uncross your arms, the knot will be formed.

194. Yes, very easily, by folding the paper and then wrinkling it as shown below.

195. Make a knot with a loop at the base of the rope, and then cut the loop. The knot will be still holding the ends of the rope.

196. First, tie the lower ends. Then climb up the first rope and cut the second one, close to the ceiling, leaving an end long enough to form a loop. (You can instead cut it off entirely if you can slide the rope through the hook.) Hanging from the loop, cut the first rope at the hook. Be careful not to drop it. Then slide the rope through the loop until it's even. Climb down the double rope and, once on the floor, pull one end to get it all.

197. Pour water in the hole a little at a time. The ball will rise until it completely comes out of the hole.

198. By releasing some air from the tires so that they lower the total height of the truck more than two inches. The truck can then easily go under the bridge.

199. By tossing it upward. First it will go up, then it will stop momentarily and start coming down following the same path.

200. By cutting the wood into two or three pieces, 20 centimeters in length. In this way, you obtain pieces with a rectangular surface of 5 by 20 centimeters and you can then put them in the hole, stopping the leak.

201. Yes, by putting on your pants inside out.

202. When you take off your shoe, I'll take off mine at the same time. That way, you are not doing it alone.

203. By pushing the cork inside the bottle.

204. By turning the box upside down and sliding the lid enough to make some diamonds fall. Then close it, turn it back to its original position, and put it back in its place.

205. The paper reads, "You will write the word 'NO' on the paper." If you write "NO," you are indicating that it will not happen, although it has really happened. If you write "YES," you are indicating that it will happen, although it actually has not happened. No matter what you write, you will not get it right.

206. Save one penny every other day. When he dies, you will have the exact amount.

207. Place the newspaper page under a closed door. Each person steps on one end of the page so that they cannot touch each other without opening the door. To open the door, they would have to step off of the paper.

208. Something that specifically involves you. For example, crawling under your legs. Your friend can crawl under your legs, but you cannot crawl under your own legs.

209. Roll up the rug (or the bill) starting on one end until it reaches the bottle. Then, continue rolling it slowly so that the bottle moves until it is entirely off the rug. During this process, only the rug is touching the bottle.

210. Always advance half the distance remaining to the wall. In this way, there will always be some distance between you and the wall. The distance left approaches zero, but it never actually reaches zero.

   If we consider d as the initial distance to the wall, the distance traveled is d x $(1/2 + 1/4 + 1/8 + 1/16 + ... + 1/2^n)$.

211. Because they placed the ballpoint pen on the ground leaning against a high wall.

212. To make the authorities think that he was going to jump with a hostage. If they thought that, they would not give him a defective parachute.

213. There were no footprints. Therefore, the man and package fell from the sky. The package was the parachute that had not opened up. That is why the man was dead.

214. He was on a long bridge, so he had to run 20 yards toward where the police car was approaching from in order to get off the bridge. Then he ran toward the forest.

215. The husband died before he woke up. Therefore, nobody could have known what he had been dreaming about.

216. The man used the ladder to tie the rope to the hook. Then, he took it out of the room and brought in a big block of ice. He stood on the block of ice to hang himself. The moisture on the floor came from the ice melting down.

217. He talked to the travel agency where the couple had bought their tickets and found out that the husband had ordered a one-way ticket for his wife and a round-trip ticket for himself.

218. He took out one marble and swallowed it before someone else could see its color. This forced the count to take out the other marble. It was black, of course, so they all assumed that the previous one had been white.

219. He dug up the dirt with his hands to form a little mound. He then stepped on the mound to reach the water.

220. The man stabbed himself with an icicle. The ice melted. This explains why there was no weapon.

221. If Albert had stopped the cassette player when the killer came in, the tape would not have been rewound. This means that the killer had listened to the tape to make sure that the imitation was perfect.

222. The killer blocked the deadbolt with a chunk of ice. When the ice melted down, the door locked itself.

223. The maid, because pages 99 and 100 are two sides of the same sheet of paper.

224. If the police detective heard the shots at the same time, it means that the men could not have died at the same time. If both sounds had occurred at the same time at opposite ends of the train, he would have first heard the one from the front car, because the speed of the train was added to the speed of sound. For the sound from the back of the train, the speed of the train was subtracted from the speed of sound. For the detective to hear both shots at once means the man at the back of the train was killed first.

225. The guilty man was one Siamese twin, and his twin was innocent.

226. New York City is in the Northern Hemisphere and Australia is in the Southern Hemisphere. Due to the earth's movement, water and air masses turn in different directions in both hemispheres. In the Southern Hemisphere, they turn clockwise, while in the Northern Hemisphere, they turn counterclockwise. When he saw the direction of the water draining from the sink, Ernest knew where he was.

227. The footprints were not very deep, which means that they could not belong to a very heavy person. Therefore, they had to belong to the secretary, who had changed shoes to hide her crime.

Both wounds must have occurred when the victim placed a hand on his chest before the gunshot and the bullet crossed his hand before going into his chest.

228. I climbed up a cherry tree that had two cherries and picked only one. I left the other one on the tree. I did not "pick cherries," because I "picked a cherry."

229. Humans. When we are little, we crawl on all fours. When we are adults, we stand on two feet. When we are old, we use a cane.

230. Silence.

231. The letter "i".

232. A shadow.

233. None. The ship floats and it always weighs the same in the water. It will rise with the tide, so its flotation line will always be the same. So the ladder will still be 22 steps.

234. Two minutes. During the first minute, the front of the train will pass through the tunnel, and during the second minute, the rest of the train will pass through the tunnel.

100 m   100 m

235. When they crossed, they were both in the same place. Therefore, they were both equidistant from Madrid.

236. The trains going to the movies arrive one minute earlier than the other ones. So if my uncle arrives at a random time, nine time out of ten the movie train will come first.

237. Two hours and thirteen minutes. (If you multiply by 60, the minutes become hours and the seconds become minutes.)

238. If you put my bird inside any supersonic plane and make it fly in the same direction as the plane, it will be going faster than the plane.

239. The top of the highest mast in the boat traveled a distance $2\pi d$ feet longer than the lowest point of the boat, which is d feet lower.

240. A bird cannot fly on the moon because there is no air to suspend the bird.

241. The passenger should sit at the end of the train and when the train enters the tunnel, he should run toward the front of the train. The time he spends in the tunnel will be shorter than if he had remained seated.

242. The combined speed of the trains is 50 + 70 = 120 miles per hour. It will take them half an hour to travel the 60 miles between them. During this time, the bird will travel 40 miles.

243. 100 inches. The stone moves relative to the log and the log to the terrain.

244. The combined speed of the trains is 80 + 120 = 200 meters per minute. One minute before crashing, they will be 200 meters apart.

245. You might think that the snail would take 200 minutes in traveling 100 centimeters, but you have to realize that at the end of the 194th minute it will be 3 centimeters away from the end. This means that in the 195th minute, the snail will reach it and will not slide down again. The answer is 195 minutes.

246. The young man took ten minutes to go to the other end of the train and back. During this time, the man's suitcases have traveled five miles. The train travels five miles every ten minutes, which makes the speed 30 miles per hour.

247. 15, counting the times that they meet at a port while one ship is leaving and the other arriving. 13, if we do not count these crossings. When the ship leaves, there are already seven ships on the way that it will come across at some point during the journey. It will also cross with the one ship that leaves when it leaves and the seven other ships that will depart during the ship's journey. The figure below represents this situation. The arrow indicates a ship that leaves New York destined for London. The dotted lines indicate the ships it passes.

248. The needle will travel approximately 9.5 centimeters (the radius of the record minus the non-playable areas, $15 - 5 - 0.5 = 9.5$ centimeters.) Actually, the speed of the record and the number of grooves do not affect the result. The needle moves in an arc of a circle whose radius is the length of the tonearm.

249. This point maintains a constant speed, independent of the length of the shadow.

250. When the card speeds up, the inertia pushes the air back inside the car, compressing the air behind the balloon and thus pushing the balloon forward. When the car turns, the balloon will move toward the inside of the turn.

251. The lower ends of the rim of the wheels. Their trajectory is shown below:

When the train goes in one direction, those points move in the opposite direction.

252. If the dog went faster than 330 meters per second (the speed of sound), it could not hear the noise of the can. So that is the fastest the dog can run.

253. Because the speed ratio was the same, runner number "1" won. We can verify this mathematically:

$$\frac{v_1}{v_2} = \frac{100}{95} = \frac{105}{x_2} \qquad\qquad x_2 = 99.75 \text{ meters}$$

254. The director got to the office 20 minutes early and he saw the car at "x" distance from his house. Then the car took 20 minutes in traveling that distance back and forth. So the director came across the car 10 minutes before his regular departure time and therefore he walked exactly 50 minutes.

255. Without the current, the boat takes 20 minutes. It goes six miles in twenty minutes, so its speed is 18 mph.

With a current D the first trip would be $V_1 = 18 - 2 = 16$ mph, taking $T_1 = {}^{D_1}/V_1 = {}^3/_{16} = 11$ minutes and 15 seconds. The return trip would be $V_2 = 18 + 2 = 20$ mph, taking $T_2 = {}^3/_{20} = 9$ minutes.

The total trip, in this case, would take 20 minutes and 15 seconds, which is more than the trip without the current.

256. There is such a spot. Let's imagine that on the same day that one person was climbing down, the other was climbing up. They must have met at a certain point of the trip. This is the spot we are looking for.

257. Two blankets one inch thick each, because the air between them also acts as insulation.

258. No. It hasn't because the total weight of the ice is equal to the volume of water moved.

259. This can never happen. These are two contradictory concepts. If one of them exists, the other cannot possibly exist as well.

260. At the North or South Pole.

261. I must pour it before going upstairs, because the coffee will lose more heat before adding the milk rather than after. (Matter loses heat proportionally to the difference in temperature with the surrounding environment.)

262. The flotation line will be lower, because the raft will be lighter. The water level of the pool will also be lower, because the volume of water that the rocks move when they are in the raft is larger than the volume of water the rocks move when they are at the bottom of the pool. When the rocks are on the raft, they move a volume of water equal to the weight of the rocks. When the rocks are at the bottom of the pool, the volume of the water moved is equal to the actual volume of the rocks. Since rocks are denser than water, this is the smaller of the two volumes.

263. The flotation line will be the same, because the weight of the boat does not change.

264. Eight times, as shown below.

265. While the raft is loaded with the salt, he must mark the flotation line. Then, he must unload the salt and load the raft with gold until the water level reaches the flotation line. This means that the weight of the salt and the gold will be equal.

266. Place the bottle horizontally and let the wine gradually pour out until the horizontal surface of the wine is at the middle of the bottle, as shown in the illustration.

267. Put pieces of glass of the broken pitcher in the pitcher containing acid until the level reaches the five-quart mark. Then pour the acid until it reaches the two-quart mark.

268. Before leaving home, he wound the clock and set it for twelve o'clock. When he got back home, he knew exactly how long he had been out because of his own clock.

At his friend's house, he checked the time. Once he was back home, he subtracted the time he was at his friend's house from the total time indicated by the clock. The remainder was used in walking to and from his friend's house. He divided this number into two and added the result to the time that he saw on his friend's clock when he was leaving his friend's house.

269. Two turns on itself. (You can actually try this yourself.)

270. Mr. Brown does not wear a brown or white tie. Therefore, it has to be red. Mr. White's tie can't be white, so it must be brown. That leaves Mr. Red with the white tie.

271. The maximum distance for the first two points is when they are on opposite ends of a circumference of that sphere. The circumference divides the sphere into two hemispheres. The third point has to be in one of these hemispheres. Therefore, it will certainly happen.

272. The puzzle says to draw a square "with two straight lines." The easiest solution is the one shown in the illustration following, which shows a square with two straight lines.

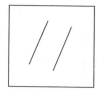

273. It is possible to predict it. That doesn't mean that he is right in his predictions.

274. This puzzle is based on an old joke. What really happened was that the young man kissed his own hand and then slapped the older man in the face.

275. There is no smoke coming out of an electric train.

276. Peacocks don't lay eggs. Peahens do.

277. A hole, for example.

278. One dozen.

279. He has a glass eye.

280. A quintet.

281. When he got married, he was a billionaire. Because of his wife's spending habits, he became a millionaire.

282. He can take out his dentures and bite his good eye with them.

283. Baby elephants.

284. During his last lap.

285. You can go in through the door.

286. The hare was lying. (The first paragraph of the puzzle gives the order.)

287. Staying up at night.

288. Wet.

289. Bicycles.

Hard-to-Solve

BRAIN TEASERS

The brainteasers in this section have two purposes: to let you have fun and to train your mind.

You don't need any special knowledge to solve them. It's a matter of thinking a little about the questions and applying common sense.

The puzzles are organized by order of difficulty. If you cannot find the answer to a problem and feel like giving up, refer to the **"Hints"** (**pages 137 through 141**) for some clues to finding the answer.

Solving these brainteasers can be a good activity for a solo player or a group, and can be turned into a game of competition.

The answers for this section can be found on pages 143 through 166.

1. TWINS

Peter and Paul are twin brothers. One of them (we don't know which) always lies. The other one always tells the truth. I ask one of them:

"Is Paul the one that lies?"

"Yes," he answers.

Did I speak to Peter or Paul?

2. TWIN STATISTICS

Suppose that 3% of births give rise to twins. What percentage of the population is a twin: 3%, less than 3%, or more than 3%?

3. PLACE YOUR CARDS

You have three cards: an ace, a queen, and a six. One is a diamond, one is a heart, and one is a spade, although not necessarily in that order.

The diamond sits between the queen and the heart.

The six is immediately to the right of the spade.

Write in the picture below where each card is located.

4. THE PROFESSOR AND HIS FRIEND

Professor Zizoloziz puts 40 matches on the table and explains a game to his friend Kathy.

Each player in turn takes one, three, or five matches. The winner is the one who takes the last match. Kathy chooses to go first and takes three matches.

Who do you think will win this game, Kathy or the professor?

5. IRREGULAR CIRCUIT

Two cars start from point A at the same time and drive around a circuit more than one mile in length. While they are driving laps around the circuit, each car must maintain a steady speed. Since one car is faster than the other, one car will pass the other at certain points. The first pass occurs 150 yards from point A.

At what distance from A will one car pass the other again?

6. ECONOMICAL PROGRESSION

Below are four terms in an arithmetic progression (a series in which the difference between terms is constant, in this case 50):

5, 55, 105, 155

Notice how the four terms use only three different digits: 0, 1, and 5.
Can you find six terms in an arithmetic progression that use only three different digits?

7. SKIN AND SHOES

A white man is wearing a pair of white shoes, a black man is wearing a pair of black shoes, and a red-skinned man is wearing a pair of red shoes. In a gesture of friendship, they decide to exchange shoes. When they are done, each man has on one shoe from each of the other two men.

How many shoes will you have to look at to know which color of shoe each man is wearing on each foot; that is, which color shoe each man wears on his right foot and which color each man wears on his left foot? Note that when you look at a shoe, you can see that man's skin color.

8. UP AND DOWN

This morning I had to take the stairs because the elevator was out of service. I had already gone down seven steps when I saw Professor Zizoloziz on the ground floor coming up. I continued descending at my usual pace, greeted the professor when we passed, and was surprised to see that when I still had four more steps to go, the professor had gone up the whole flight. "When I go down one step, he goes up two," I thought.

How many steps does the staircase have?

9. WHAT MONTH—I

A month begins on a Friday and ends on a Friday, too. What month is it?

10. WHAT MONTH—II

The result of adding the date of the last Monday of last month and the date of the first Thursday of next month is 38. If both dates are of the same year, what is the current month?

11. EVE'S ENIGMA

After heaven, the earth, the grass, and all the animals were created, the snake, who was very smart, decided to make its own contribution.

It decided to lie every Tuesday, Thursday, and Saturday. For the other days of the week, it told the truth.

"Eve, dear Eve, why don't you try an apple?" the snake suggested.

"But I am not allowed to!" said Eve.

"Oh, no!" said the snake. "You can eat it today since it is Saturday and God is resting."

"No, not today," said Eve, "Maybe tomorrow."

"Tomorrow is Wednesday and it will be too late," insisted the snake.

This is how the snake tricked Eve.

What day of the week did this conversation take place?

12. BROKEN M

We have formed six triangles by drawing three straight lines on the M. That's not enough. Starting with a new M, form nine triangles by drawing three straight lines.

13. SOCCER SCORES—I

A soccer tournament has just ended. Five teams participated and each one played once against each of the other teams. The winner of a match received 2 points, the losing team 0 points, and each team received 1 point for a tie.

The final results were:
Lions   6 points
Tigers   5 points
Bears   3 points
Orioles   1 point

We are missing one team, the Eagles. What was their point total?

14. SOCCER SCORES—II

In a three-team tournament, each team played once against each of the two other teams. Each team scored one goal.

The final results were:
Lions   3 points
Tigers   2 points
Bears   1 point

What was the score in each match?

15. WHAT TIME IS IT—I

I'm looking at my watch. From this moment on, the hour hand will take exactly twice as long as the minute hand to reach the number 6. What time is it?

16. WHAT TIME IS IT—II

I'm looking at my watch. From this moment on, the hour hand will take exactly three times longer than the minute hand to reach the number 6. What time is it?

17. WHAT TIME IS IT—III

I'm looking at my watch. The hour hand is on one mark and the minute hand is on the next one. (By marks, we mean minute marks.) What time is it?

18. WHAT TIME IS IT—IV

I'm looking at my watch. The hour hand is on one mark and the minute hand is on the previous one. (By marks, we mean minute marks.) What time is it?

19. PROHIBITED CONNECTION

Using the numbers 1, 2, 3, 4, 5, and 6, put each of them in a circle. There is only one condition. The circles connected by a line cannot have consecutive numbers. For example, 4 cannot be connected with 3 or 5.

20. CONCENTRIC

The big square has an area of 60 square inches. Is there a fast way to figure out what the area of the small square is?

21. JOHN CASH

John Cash saw his face on a poster nailed to a tree. As he approached, he saw "WANTED, DEAD OR ALIVE." Under his picture, it read "REWARD:____DOLLARS."

There was a three-digit figure on the poster. John drew his Colt and shot at the first number (in the hundreds column).

He had just reduced the price on his head by five times.

"Good Lord!" said the doctor's daughter, who was sitting on the other side of the tree doing her math homework.

John blushed, and shot again at another number (in the tens column).

He had just reduced the price on his head by another five times.

"Nice shooting!" said the young girl.

"Thank you, miss," said John. He spurred his horse and never returned.

What was the initial reward offered on John's head?

22. RUSSIAN ROULETTE

Russian roulette was created by Count Ugo Lombardo Fiumiccino, who successfully died during his first presentation of it.

He placed six jars on a shelf, as in the drawing below. After staring at them, he closed his eyes and told his friend to fill them up with the ingredients, making sure that each jar contained an ingredient other than the one shown on its label.

When she was finished, the count asked:

"Dear Petrushka, would you be so kind as to tell me where the salt is?"

"Under the jar containing snuff," answered Petrushka.

"My dear friend, would you tell me where the sugar is?" he asked.

"Immediately to the right of the jar containing coffee," she answered.

Ugo Lombardo Fiumiccino, confirming his desire to commit suicide, reached immediately for the jar containing arsenic.

Where is the arsenic?

23. NEW RACE

Two cars start traveling from two different points and in opposite directions in a circuit race at a constant speed. The cars cross for the first time at point A. The second time is at point B. The third time is at point C, and the fourth one is again at point A.

How much faster is one car going than the other?

24. THE CALCULATOR KEYS

Several times Professor Zizoloziz mentioned that he feels uncomfortable looking at his pocket calculator. Yesterday, he was elated because he had found the reason why. The layout of the keys from 1 to 9 and the "minus" and "equal" signs look like they are doing subtraction. It's an incorrect equation, however, because 789 minus 456 does not equal 123. Zizoloziz thought of changing the numbers to achieve a correct equation. He changed 7 with 3, then 3 with 4, and 9 with 6, resulting in 486 − 359 = 127. He made only three changes to achieve this.

Using the keyboard below as a reference, can you obtain a correctly subtracted number with only two changes?

25. NICE DISCOUNTS

A bookstore has a nice discount policy. If you buy a $20 book today, you get a 2% discount on your next purchase. If you buy a $15 book, you get a 1.5% discount on your next purchase. If you have to buy three books that cost $10, $20, and $30, you could buy the $30 book today, the $10 book tomorrow (on which you'll get a 3% discount), and the $20 book the following day (on which you'll get a 1% discount). Or you could buy the $30 book and the $20 book today, and the $10 book tomorrow (with a 5% discount).

What is the cheapest way to buy five books priced at $10, $20, $30, $40, and $50?

26. ENIGMATIC FARES

Professor Zizoloziz always adds the five digits on a bus transfer. Yesterday, he rode route 62 with a friend. As soon as he got the tickets, which were consecutively numbered, he added the numbers on them and then told his friend that the sum of all ten digits was exactly 62. His logical friend asked him if the sum of the numbers on either of the tickets was by any chance 35. Professor Zizoloziz answered and his friend then knew the numbers on the bus tickets.

What were the numbers on the two bus tickets?

27. HOROSCOPE

An indiscreet young man asks his beautiful mathematics teacher her age. She responds, "Today's date is my age, although before this week is over there will be another day with a date one fifth of the new age that I will be."

What is the teacher's sign of the zodiac?

28. STRANGERS IN THE NIGHT

The midnight train is coming down the Strujen-Bajen mountains. Art Farnanski seems to be dozing off in his seat.

Someone knows that this is not true.

At the station, all the passengers get off the train, except one. The conductor comes and taps him on the shoulder to let him know they have arrived. Art Farnanski does not answer. He is dead.

"His heart?" asks Commander Abrojos, looking at the dead body.

"Strychnine," answers the forensic doctor.

Hours later, the four people that had shared the train compartment with the dead man are at the police station.

The man in the dark suit:
"I'm innocent. The blonde woman was talking to Farnanski."

The blonde woman:
"I'm innocent. I did not speak to Farnanski."

The man in the light suit:
"I'm innocent. The brunette woman killed him."

The brunette woman:
"I'm innocent. One of the men killed him."

That same morning, while he is serving him coffee, the waiter at the Petit Piccolo asks Commander Abrojos:

"This is an easy case for you, isn't it?"

"Yes," answers the Commander. "Four true statements and four false ones. Easy as pie."

Who killed Farnanski? (Only one person is guilty.)

29. MONTE CARLO

The famous playboy Hystrix Tardigradus explained to a beautiful woman his system for playing roulette:

"In each round, I always bet half of the money I have at the time on red. Yesterday, I counted and I had won as many rounds as I had lost."

Over the course of the night, did Hystrix win, lose, or break even?

30. THE FOREIGNERS AND THE MENU

A particular inn always offers the same nine dishes on its dinner menu: A, B, C, D, E, F, G, H, and I.

Five foreigners arrive. Nobody tells them which dish corresponds to which letter and so they each select one letter without knowing what they will eat.

The innkeeper arrives with the five dishes ordered and puts them in the center of the table so that they can decide who eats what.

This goes on for two more nights.

The foreigners, who are professors of logic, are able to deduce by the dishes they ordered which letter represents which dish.

What could have been the dishes ordered each of the three nights?

31. FORT KNOX JUMPING FROGS—I

The first puzzle of this series is very well known. We included it here, though, because it is good practice for the following puzzles, since they all use the same method of moving coins.

Make a line of eight coins. In four moves, make four piles of two coins each.

A move consists of taking one coin, skipping over two others, and piling it on top of the next one.

The answers list one of several possible solutions for all of the puzzles in this series.

32. FORT KNOX JUMPING FROGS—II

Place 14 coins in the shape of a cross, as shown in the illustration. In seven moves as described in Puzzle 31, make seven piles of two coins each. Note: Only move the coins in a straight line; do not change directions.

33. FORT KNOX JUMPING FROGS—III

Place 12 coins on the three rings as shown in the illustration below. In six moves as described in Puzzle 31, make six piles of two coins each. Note: Only move the coins around their own rings and always go clockwise in direction.

34. FORT KNOX JUMPING FROGS—IV

Place 20 coins in the shape of a star as shown in the illustration below. In ten moves as described in Puzzle 31, make ten piles of two coins each. Note: Only move the coins along the straight lines and do not turn corners.

35. FORT KNOX JUMPING FROGS—V

Place 20 coins in a 4 x 5 rectangle as shown below. In ten moves as described in Puzzle 31, make ten piles of two coins each. Note: Coins can move only in a straight line and cannot move diagonally.

36. THE HAREM

The story goes that the harem of the Great Tamerlane was protected by a door with many locks. The vizier and four slaves were in charge of guarding this door.

Knowledgeable of the weaknesses of men, the Great Tamerlane had distributed the keys in such a way that the vizier could only open the door if he was with any one of the slaves, and the slaves could only open it if three of them worked together.

How may locks did the door have?

37. THE DIVIDING END

My ID number is quite remarkable. It's a nine-digit number with each of the digits from 1 to 9 appearing once. The whole number is divisible by 9. If you remove the rightmost digit, the remaining eight-digit number is divisible by 8. Removing the next rightmost digit leaves a seven-digit number that is divisible by 7. This property continues all the way down to one digit. What is my ID number?

38. THE ISLAND AND THE ENGLISHMEN

On a deserted island (except for a small group of Englishmen) there are four clubs.

The membership lists reveal that:
a) Each Englishman is a member of two clubs.
b) Every set of two clubs has only one member in common.
How many Englishmen are there on the island?

39. LOGIC APPLES

Four perfect logicians, who all knew each other from being members of the Perfect Logicians' Club, sat around a table that had a dish with 11 apples in it. The chat was intense, and they ended up eating all the apples. Everybody had at least one apple, and everyone knew that fact, and each logician knew the number of apples that he ate. They didn't know how many apples each of the others ate, though. They agreed to ask only questions that they didn't know the answers to:

Alonso: Did you eat more apples than I did, Bertrand?
Bertrand: I don't know. Did you, George, eat more apples than I did?
George: I don't know.
Kurt: Aha!

Kurt figured out how many apples each person ate. Can you do the same?

40. ADDED CORNERS

Using the numbers from 1 to 8, place one in each shape with one condition: The number in each square has to be the sum of its two neighboring circles.

105

41. RECTANGLES

The vertical rectangle (solid line) has an area of 40 square inches.
Find out in a quick way the area of the inclined rectangle (dotted line).

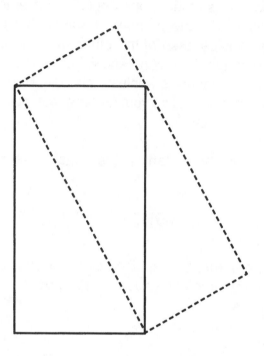

42. A WARM FAREWELL

At a train station, the Porter family is saying good-bye to the Robinson family. We don't know who is leaving and who is staying.

Each of the members of the Porter family say farewell to each of the members of the Robinson family. To say good-bye, two men shake hands, and both a man and a woman and two women kiss once on the cheek.

An eyewitness to the event counted 21 handshakes and 34 kisses.
How many men and how many women were saying good-bye?

43. FOUR MINUS ONE IS A CRIME

Messrs. A, B, C, and D met last night in a corner in the circled area. After the meeting, each of them went home, except for one, Mr. D, who was discovered dead this morning in the river.

"Did you take the statements from the three suspects?"

"Yes, commissioner. Mr. A declared that from the corner of the meeting he walked seven blocks to get home. Mr. B said that he walked six blocks to get home. Mr. C answered that he walked five blocks to get home. I marked their homes on the map."

"And in which corner did they meet?"

"Nobody remembers."

"Do you want to know something? It isn't necessary, because I know that one of the three suspects is lying."

"And that is the killer!"

"Brilliant deduction!"

Who is the killer?

44. ON THE ROUTE OF MARCO POLO

On his way east, Marco Polo passed five little villages along a straight road. At each village a road sign points to one of the other four villages. Below are the five signs, in no particular order. Can you add the corresponding arrows to the four signs that have lost them?
(The five signs are all on the same side of the road.)

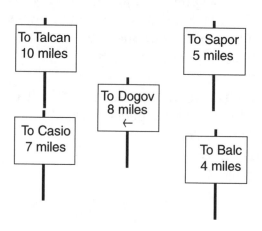

45. ON THE ROAD

On my way to Philadelphia, I pass five mileposts that indicate their respective distances to Philadelphia. The mileposts are at fixed intervals. What's curious is that each milepost has a two-digit number, and together the five mileposts use all the digits from 0 to 9 once.
What is the smallest distance that the closest milepost can be from Philadelphia? (As usual, mileposts don't begin with 0.)

46. TOUCHING SQUARES

Shown here are three squares on a table with each one touching the other two squares. If you want to place squares so that each square touches exactly three other squares (not counting corner-to-corner or corner-to-side contact), how may squares do you need? All squares must lie on the table surface.

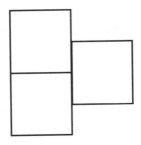

47. EQUAL VISION

Each watchman looks in all directions (horizontal, vertical, and diagonal). On the left board, each watchman has five vacant cells under his gaze. (A watchman can see beyond another watchman.) On the right, each watchman can see six empty cells. What's the maximum number of watchmen that can be placed so that each sees seven empty cells?

48. BLOOD AND SAND

"You are the killer!" declared Commissioner Abrojos. His assistant, Inspector Begonias, slanted his eyes and looked around. They were alone in the room.

"I don't understand," he said.

"You are the killer!" the commissioner repeated.

Here is the story:

Yesterday, responding to a phone call, Inspector Begonias visited the mansion of millionaire Lincoln Dustin at around 7 p.m. The millionaire was dead in his office. There were bloodstains on the carpet around the desk. Begonias inspected the place. He questioned the butler, who told him that Lincoln Dustin always led a perfectly ordered life. Every day, at noon, Mr. Dustin started the hourglass, the one that was now next to his dead body. At exactly midnight, the hourglass finished and Lincoln Dustin would go to sleep.

Begonias thought this was all very interesting, but not so useful for his investigation. That same night, the butler's call woke him up.

"Inspector!" cried the butler, "The hourglass did not finish at midnight, but at 3 a.m.!"

Begonias told all of this to Commissioner Abrojos.

"Let's suppose," said the commissioner, "that Mr. Dustin was able to turn the hourglass to leave us a clue as to the time of the crime."

Begonias nodded.

"In that case," continued the commissioner, "you told me that you had gone to the mansion around 7 p.m., which makes me think that you are the killer."

This is how they reached the conversation at the beginning of our puzzle.

Begonias could not believe it.

"I never thought," he said sadly, "that you would do this to me."

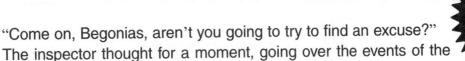

"Come on, Begonias, aren't you going to try to find an excuse?"

The inspector thought for a moment, going over the events of the previous day.

"The hourglass!" he cried. "I remember now. When I inspected the room I saw that the hourglass was on a handwritten note."

"Do you mean that the victim wrote the name of the killer? I don't believe that."

"Not at all!" said Begonias. "I wanted to read the note, so I lifted the hourglass and then I must have turned it upside down by mistake."

"What time was it then?"

"7 p.m."

"My dear friend, this clears you as a suspect!" said the commissioner.

Suppose that Mr. Dustin was able to invert the hourglass before dying. At what time did he die? Why did the commissioner consider Begonias a suspect?

49. INTERNATIONAL SUMMIT

At a recent international summit, five delegates (A, B, C, D, and E) participated. This is what we observed:

1. B and C spoke English, although when D joined them, they all changed to Spanish, the only common language among the three of them.

2. The only common language among A, B, and E was French.

3. The only common language between C and E was Italian.

4. Three delegates could speak Portuguese.

5. The most common language was Spanish.

6. One of the delegates spoke all five languages, another one spoke four, one spoke three, one spoke two, and the other only spoke one language.

What languages did each delegate speak?

50. MISTER DIGIT FACE

Place each of the digits 1 to 9, one digit per blank, so that the product of the two eyes equals the number above the head, and the product of each eye and mouth equals the number on the respective side of the face.

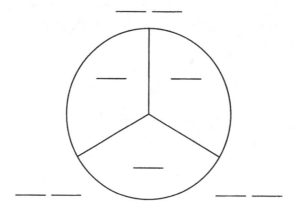

51. DIGIT TREE

Using each digit from 1 to 9 once, make seven numbers so that each number is equal to the sum of the numbers in the circles that are connected to it from below. (The numbers can be more than one digit.) There are two slightly different answers.

52. FIGURES TO CUT IN TWO

Each one of the following figures can be divided into two equal parts (that may be mirror images of each other). The dividing lines can follow the grid or not. The grid is only to provide proportion to the figures.

53. SEGMENTS

Place the digits 1 to 9 (using each digit once, one digit per box) so that:
- The boxes containing the 1 and 2 and all the ones between them add up to 12.

- The boxes containing the 2 and 3 and all the ones between them add up to 23.

- The boxes containing the 3 and 4 and all the ones between them add up to 34.

- The boxes containing the 4 and 5 and all the ones between them add up to 45.

54. MULTIPLE TOWERS

As the elevator rises along the eight-floor tower, it forms a series of three-digit numbers by combining the 72 in the elevator with the digit on the floor. What's more, these three-digit numbers are multiples of 2, 3, 4, etc., up to 9. (That is, on the lowest floor, 726 is evenly divisible by 2; on the next floor, 723 is evenly divisible by 3, and so on.) Can you find another arrangement for the digits 0 to 9 (using each digit once, one digit per box) so that the elevator isn't 72 and the combinations of the elevator with the level form an appropriate multiple?

55. EARTHLINGS

August 2002.

The spaceship landed.

"Earth!" they shouted.

They knew that earthlings are divided into three groups: those who always tell the truth, those who always lie, and those who do both, alternating between true and false statements, starting with either.

"Let's go!" said the captain.

The aliens approached three earthlings, who each were from a different group, and asked, "Who won the last World Cup? Who came in second? Who came in third?"

One of them responded, "Zaire first. Uruguay second. Spain third."

Another one said, "Zaire first. Spain second. Uruguay third."

The third one said, "Uruguay first. Spain second. Zaire third."

The aliens returned to their spaceship and flew back to where they came from.

Do you know which response was the true ranking in the World Cup?

56. THE ANT AND THE CLOCK

Precisely when the big hand of the clock passes 12, an ant begins crawling counterclockwise around the clock from the 6 mark at a consistent speed.

When reaching the big hand of the clock, the ant turns around and, at the same speed, starts marching around the clock in the opposite direction.

Exactly 45 minutes after the first meeting, the ant crosses the big hand for the second time.

How long has the ant been walking?

57. HIDDEN WORD—I

A four-letter word belongs in the rectangle below. You are given several clues to help guess what it is.

In the column marked "2," you have words that share exactly two letters in the same position as the hidden word. For example, if the hidden word were REDO, in column 2 we could put DEMO, BEDS, DODO, etc. Column 1 contains words that share exactly one letter in the same position as the hidden word. In the example above, REDO being the hidden word, column 1 could have NODS, ROAD, etc.

Column 0 has words that do not share any letter in the same position as the hidden word. For our example, column 0 could have GAME, HARD, etc.

Now find the hidden word.

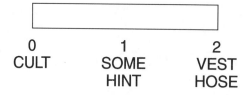

0	1	2
CULT	SOME	VEST
	HINT	HOSE

58. HIDDEN WORD—II

A three-letter word belongs in the rectangle below. Given the words below, figure out what it is.

0	1	2
HAS	CON	SON
	CAB	

59. HIDDEN WORD—III

A five-letter word belongs in the rectangle below. Given the words below, figure out what it is.

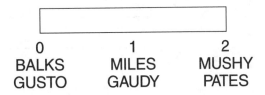

0	1	2
BALKS	MILES	MUSHY
GUSTO	GAUDY	PATES

SECRET NUMBER

In the first field of the first row of every illustration we have written (in invisible ink) a number formed by four different digits between 0 and 9.

The following rows indicate attempts to find out the secret number. Each try has, in the column to the right, its grade with letters R (right) and B (bingo). Each R indicates that this number has one digit in common with the secret number, but in a different position. Each B indicates that the number has one digit in common with the secret number in the same position.

Find out the secret number in the following tables.

60. SECRET NUMBER—I

				B	B	B	B
8	9	5	1	R	R		
2	1	6	9	R	B		
3	6	9	4	R	B		
4	7	2	1	R	B		
1	2	3	7	R	R	R	

61. SECRET NUMBER—II

				B	B	B	B
6	2	5	3	R			
8	1	4	7	R	R		
2	5	7	1	B			
3	6	0	9	R	R		
9	6	8	7	B	B		

62. SECRET NUMBER—III

				B	B	B	B
1	0	2	9	R			
3	4	6	2	R	R		
5	8	4	9	R	R		
8	5	2	1	R	R		
4	2	8	5	R	R	R	

63. SECRET NUMBER—IV

				B	B	B	B
3	9	2	0	R	R	R	
8	7	4	5	B			
9	0	7	5	R	R		
8	3	9	7	R	R	R	

64. SECRET NUMBER—V

				B	B	B	B
1	2	5	9	R			
1	3	8	9	R	B		
1	3	5	7	B	B		
4	3	9	7	B	B		

DOMINOES

Each one of the following diagrams uses the 28 dominoes of a domino set to make a table. The values of each domino are written down in numbers instead of in dots, but we have not identified the individual dominoes. That's exactly what you'll have to do. In the first tables, we have helped you with some of them.

Notice that each table contains the 28 dominoes and no tile appears twice in the same table. Below each table you will find a list of the 28 dominoes so that you can track what you have found and what you are still missing.

(Dominoes was created by Mr. Lech Pijanovsky, from Poland.)

65. TABLE 1

Find the 28 dominoes.

1	5	5	3	0	6	0	6
5	4	4	2	4	4	6	2
2	6	0	1	1	2	5	1
4	3	5	5	3	2	6	0
0	3	0	3	3	3	1	0
5	2	6	2	3	6	0	1
4	5	6	4	1	4	2	1

Here is a list of the 28 dominoes:

0-0						
0-1	1-1					
0-2	1-2	2-2				
0-3	1-3	2-3	3-3			
0-4	1-4	2-4	3-4	4-4		
0-5	1-5	2-5	3-5	4-5	5-5	
0-6	1-6	2-6	3-6	4-6	5-6	6-6

66. TABLE II

Find the 28 dominoes.

3	1	2	2	6	1	3	4
5	5	3	4	0	5	3	2
2	6	5	1	1	2	0	0
1	1	0	6	0	3	3	0
0	6	4	3	6	5	4	5
3	2	5	4	0	1	6	2
5	4	6	4	2	4	6	1

Here is a list of the 28 dominoes:
0-0
0-1   1-1
0-2   1-2   2-2
0-3   1-3   2-3   3-3
0-4   1-4   2-4   3-4   4-4
0-5   1-5   2-5   3-5   4-5   5-5
0-6   1-6   2-6   3-6   4-6   5-6   6-6

67. TABLE III

Find the 28 dominoes.

1	0	2	2	3	6	5
1	6	6	4	3	6	5
2	3	5	0	1	4	6
0	4	3	0	2	4	0
3	6	5	4	5	4	1
0	0	5	1	3	1	2
3	6	2	2	5	3	2
1	1	4	0	4	6	5

Here is a list of the 28 dominoes:

0-0						
0-1	1-1					
0-2	1-2	2-2				
0-3	1-3	2-3	3-3			
0-4	1-4	2-4	3-4	4-4		
0-5	1-5	2-5	3-5	4-5	5-5	
0-6	1-6	2-6	3-6	4-6	5-6	6-6

68. TABLE IV

Find the 28 dominoes.

5	4	2	3	6	3	4
4	6	5	5	0	6	3
4	6	2	3	4	1	2
6	0	6	3	0	4	1
0	6	0	2	3	4	2
5	5	6	1	4	5	3
5	1	3	2	2	1	1
1	5	2	0	1	0	0

Here is a list of the 28 dominoes:
0-0
0-1   1-1
0-2   1-2   2-2
0-3   1-3   2-3   3-3
0-4   1-4   2-4   3-4   4-4
0-5   1-5   2-5   3-5   4-5   5-5
0-6   1-6   2-6   3-6   4-6   5-6   6-6

69. TABLE V

Find the 28 dominoes.

4	0	0	1	1	1	0
5	2	3	5	6	5	6
3	5	4	4	3	4	2
2	0	0	5	6	5	3
2	2	1	5	6	0	1
2	4	4	3	2	6	4
5	6	0	3	2	3	6
1	1	3	6	4	1	0

Here is a list of the 28 dominoes:

```
0-0
0-1   1-1
0-2   1-2   2-2
0-3   1-3   2-3   3-3
0-4   1-4   2-4   3-4   4-4
0-5   1-5   2-5   3-5   4-5   5-5
0-6   1-6   2-6   3-6   4-6   5-6   6-6
```

70. TABLE VI

Find the 28 dominoes.

4	5	1	6	0	5	1
2	5	3	5	3	6	5
6	2	0	4	2	2	6
6	6	2	0	5	3	3
3	1	1	2	3	6	4
4	0	3	1	0	0	4
4	1	2	1	4	5	3
5	1	2	0	0	4	6

Here is a list of the 28 dominoes:
0-0
0-1   1-1
0-2   1-2   2-2
0-3   1-3   2-3   3-3
0-4   1-4   2-4   3-4   4-4
0-5   1-5   2-5   3-5   4-5   5-5
0-6   1-6   2-6   3-6   4-6   5-6   6-6

71. HOUND—I

A hound started on a square numbered 1, and moved from square to square numbering them in succession to the last one, numbered 20. The hound moved horizontally and vertically only, never entering any square twice. The numbers were then deleted. All we know is that the squares with circles had the numbers 5, 10, and 15, in some order. Figure out the path of the hound.

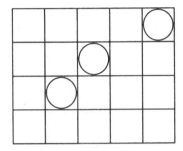

72. HOUND—II

A hound started on a square numbered 1, and moved from square to square numbering them in succession to the last one, numbered 35. The hound moved horizontally and vertically only, never entering any square twice. The numbers were then deleted. All we know is that the squares with circles had the numbers 7, 14, 21, 28, and 35, in some order. Figure out the path of the hound.

73. HOUND—III

A hound started on a square numbered 1, and moved from square to square numbering them in succession to the last one, numbered 25. The hound never entered any square twice and moved horizontally and vertically only, except for one diagonal move to a neighboring square. All the numbers except those shown were then deleted. Figure out the path of the hound.

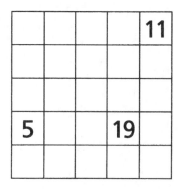

74. HOUND—IV

A hound started on a square numbered 1, and moved from square to square numbering them in succession to the last one, numbered 25. The hound never entered any square twice and moved horizontally and vertically only, except for one jump move like a chess knight, shown below left. All the numbers except those shown were then deleted. Figure out the path of the hound.

75. HOUND—V

A hound started on a square numbered 1, and moved from square to square numbering them in succession to the last one, numbered 9. The hound never entered any square twice and moved horizontally and vertically only. The prime numbers in the grid formed a symmetric pattern. Figure out the path of the hound in the bigger board where the prime numbers (2, 3, 5, 7, 11, 13, 17, 19, and 23) form a symmetric pattern. One number has been supplied. There are two answers.

POKER

We have a set of 28 poker cards (with 8, 9, 10, J, Q, K, and A). We select 25 and make a 5 x 5 table, like in the drawings.

We then have twelve "hands" of five cards (five horizontally, five vertically, and two diagonally). Next to each "hand" we write its combination.

Pair: two cards of the same value.

Two pair: two pairs plus a fifth card.

Three of a kind: three cards of equal value.

Full house: three of a kind with a pair.

Four of a kind: four cards of the same value.

Straight: five cards of consecutive values. The ace can be high or low, so the possible combinations of a straight are: A-8-9-10-J, 8-9-10-J-Q, 9-10-J-Q-K, and 10-J-Q-K-A.

Straight flush: a straight where all the cards are of the same suit.

(We write "nothing" when we have none of these combinations.)

Important: The cards of each "hand" do not have to be in order. For example, the line containing the straight can have a 9, then an 8, then a J, then a 10, then an A.

Find the values (just the values, not the suits) of all cards left blank.

76. POKER—1

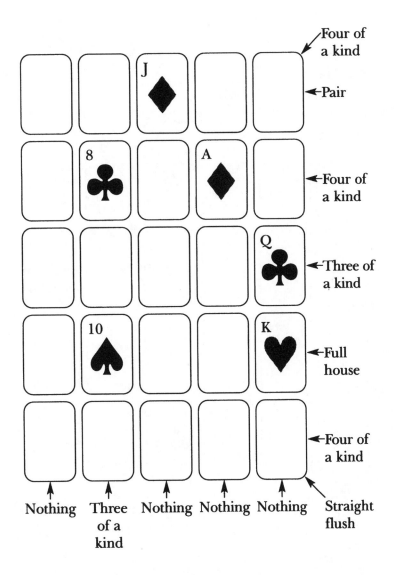

Find the values (just the values, not the suits) of all cards left blank.

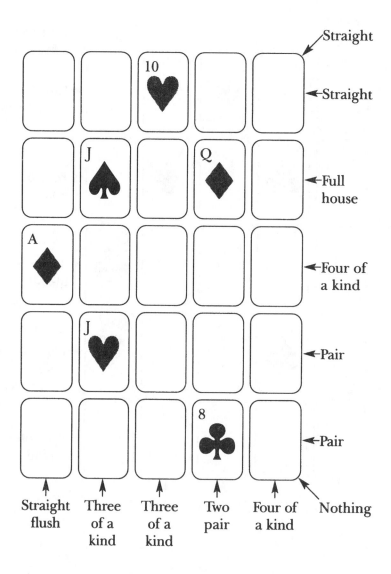

Find the values (just the values, not the suits) of all cards left blank.

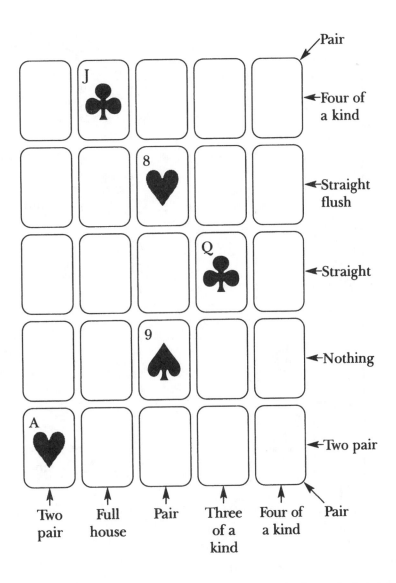

Find the values (just the values, not the suits) of all cards left blank.

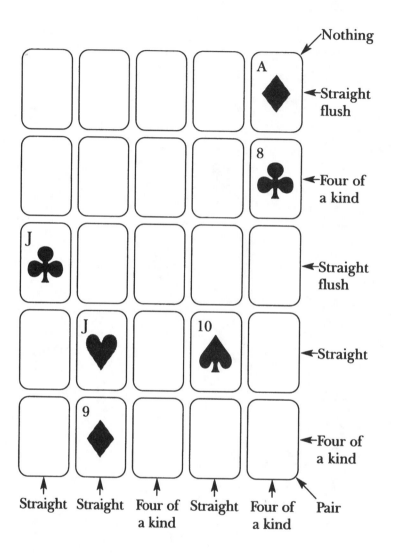

Find the values (just the values, not the suits) of all cards left blank.

80. POKER—V

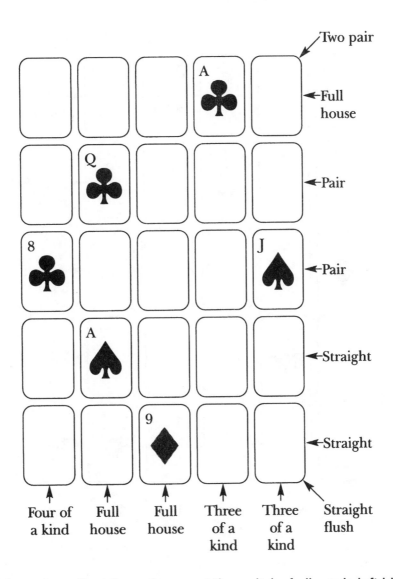

Find the values (just the values, not the suits) of all cards left blank.

81. POKER—VI

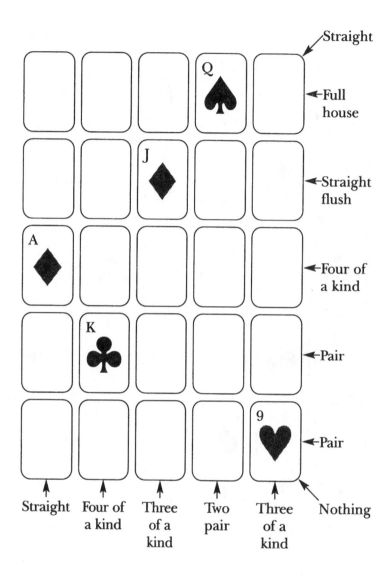

Find the values (just the values, not the suits) of all cards left blank.

Hints

Here are clues to help solve the problems.

1. **Twins.** If a person always lies or always tells the truth, can he call himself a liar?

2. **Twin Statistics.** Imagine there are 100 births, with 3% being twin births. How many people are born?

3. **Place Your Cards.** Place the diamond by following the first clue given in the puzzle. You can now tell what the queen's suit is.

4. **The Professor and His Friend.** Did you notice that each player takes an odd number of matches?

5. **Irregular Circuit.** Why not take the first pass as a new starting point?

6. **Economical Progression.** The three digits are 1, 2, and 6.

7. **Skin and Shoes.** Look at one foot and count the rest.

8. **Up and Down.** The professor had an advantage of 11 steps and is climbing at twice my speed.

9. **What Month—I.** It must be a strange month, right?

10. **What Month—II.** Note that 38 is a very high number for the sum of the first Thursday of the month and of the last Monday of another month. What days could give such a high result?

11. **Eve's Enigma.** The snake tells Eve that today is Saturday and tomorrow is Wednesday. Isn't that odd? On what days of the week can the snake talk like that?

12. **Broken M.** It might be useful to draw three straight lines on a white piece of paper and then draw an M on top of them.

13. **Soccer Scores—I.** How many games were played in the tournament? How many points in total were there in the entire tournament?

14. **Soccer Scores—II.** What were the scores for the games played by the Lions? What were the scores for the Bears?

15–18. **What Time Is It.** Think of a time, say, three o'clock. Are the conditions of the problem true for the time you just thought of? In what area of the clock are we closer to the conditions of the puzzle?

19. **Prohibited Connection.** Notice that the number 1 can be connected with four other digits. This does not occur for 2, 3, 4, or 5.

20. **Concentric.** Move the figure. What happens when you rotate the small square?

21. **John Cash.** When John erased the first number, there was a two-digit number left. Think about it. If you remove the number in the tens column, this two-digit number is divided by five.

22. **Russian Roulette.** By the first answer you know that the snuff/salt pair is vertical. Can it be on the right side? Remember that a jar never contains the ingredient shown on the label.

23. **New Race.** Take A as the starting point.

24. **The Calculator Keys.** This puzzle has two solutions. Give it a try.

25. **Nice Discounts.** Buy all the books in just two days.

26. **Enigmatic Fares.** The tickets have consecutive numbers. The sum of the digits of both is 62, an even number. What is the last digit of the first ticket?

27. **Horoscope.** Without doubt, this is a very special date.

28. **Strangers in the Night.** There are exactly four true statements. Only one person is guilty. What does this mean about the "I'm innocent" statements?

29. **Monte Carlo.** Let's say that you start with $100. If you lose and win, what happens to your money?

30. **The Foreigners and the Menu.** Out of the five dishes they order each night, could it be that two of them are the same?

31–35. **Fort Knox Jumping Frogs.** Play with some coins.

36. **The Harem.** Try it. If the door had three locks, could the Great Tamerlane's system work?

37. **The Dividing End.** Let's call the ID number ABCDEFGHI. ABCDE can be divided evenly by 5, so we know what E is.

38. **The Island and the Englishmen.** Draw four circles that represent the clubs. Connect the clubs to the members.

39. **Logic Apples.** Alonso would not have asked the question if he had eaten five or more apples, because nobody could have eaten more than he did.

40. **Added Corners.** Place the 8 first. Can it be in a corner?

41. **Rectangles.** Find a simple way to divide the figure.

42. **A Warm Farewell.** Add the number of handshakes and kisses. It comes to a total of 55. If each Porter said good-bye to each Robinson, the number of the Porter family members multiplied by the number of the Robinson family members must equal 55.

43. **Four Minus One Is a Crime.** Go from A to B on the map. Try different routes. Count how many blocks you travel every time. Compare it with the suspects' statements.

44. **On the Route of Marco Polo.** Each sign points to a different village. What can be said of the sum of the distances in each direction?

45. **On the Road.** From one sign to the next the tens' column must change.

46. **Touching Squares.** You'll need more than ten squares.

47. **Equal Vision.** It can be done with three or four watchmen. Can you do it with more?

48. **Blood and Sand.** Why did the commissioner suspect Begonias? Put yourself in his shoes. You do not know that Begonias inverted the hourglass, but instead you believe that Lincoln Dustin did it when dying.

49. **International Summit.** Use the table below. B and C speak English. Put an X in rows B and C in the English column. D doesn't speak English. Put an O in the D row in the English column.

	Eng.	Sp.	Fr.	Port.	Ital.
A					
B	X				
C	X				
D	O				
E					

50. **Mister Digit Face.** Where can 9 go?

51. **Digit Tree.** With the nine digits we have to make seven numbers. Two numbers will have two digits each. What is the highest number that could be at the top of the tree?

52. **Figures to Cut in Two.** Try several times. There is no definite way. It's a matter of eyesight.

53. **Segments.** The sum of all nine digits is 45.

54. **Multiple Towers.** Certain levels must have even numbers.

55. **Earthlings.** The second earthling had one answer in common with the first one and one in common with the third. Is this earthling honest, a liar, or both?

56. **The Ant and the Clock.** Draw a clock. Draw the path of the ant. Compare distances.

57–59. **Hidden Word.** Compare the words in column 0 with the others. If one letter appears in the same position in column 0 and also in another, you can cross it out in that column, since you know it will not be in the word in the rectangle.

60–64. **Secret Number.** When you know that a digit is not in the secret number, cross it out. If you discover that a digit is in the secret number, but don't know where, circle it. When you find its correct position, mark it with a square. Do this for all lines. Make a list of the digits that are definitely in the secret number, another for those that are not in the secret number, and a third list for those you are not sure about.

65–70. **Dominoes.** Cross out the dominoes that are already placed in the list. Let's imagine that the domino 3-4 has already been placed. Separate every other instance of 3 and 4 together in the table (remember, dominoes only appear once). Then look for pairs of numbers that are together (like 5 and 6, for example) and do the same. As you go from one puzzle to the next, you will think of more strategies.

71. **Hound–I.** If you think of the distances between the marked squares you can place the number 10. Think of where the odd and even numbers go.

72. **Hound—II.** The lower left box is 21.

73. **Hound–III.** The lower left box is 25.

74. **Hound–IV.** The lower left box is 1.

75. **Hound–V.** We have nine prime numbers. To obtain a symmetric figure, we must have the same quantity of prime numbers on the left as on the right. If we paint the board like a checkerboard with a black diagonal, we will have 12 white squares and 13 black ones. Where do the prime numbers go?

76–81. **Poker.** The straight combinations are the most useful information for you at first, especially the straight flushes. Four of a kind is also useful. Remember that all straights must have a 10 and a J, and that a four of a kind has four cards of equal value. If for a certain card you have two possible values, consider each value individually until you find the solution.

Answers

1. **Twins**

   I spoke to Peter. If a person always lies or, alternately, always tells the truth, he cannot admit that he is lying (if this person were a liar, he would be telling the truth, and if this person were honest, he would be lying). Therefore, Paul could not have answered my question. Peter could answer about Paul without contradicting himself. What we don't know is who the liar is.

2. **Twin Statistics**

   More than 3% of the population are twins. Out of 100 births, 97 are single and 3 are twins. That's 103 babies in total, 6 of which are twins, which represents 5.8% of the population.

3. **Place Your Cards**

   From left to right: queen of spades, six of diamonds, and ace of hearts.

4. **The Professor and His Friend**

   Professor Zizoloziz wins. Every player takes an odd number of matches per play. After the first player goes, there will always be an odd number of matches left. After the second player goes, there will always be an even number of matches left. Therefore, the second player is the winner.

5. **Irregular Circuit**

   300 yards from point A. The first passing point can be considered a new starting point. Therefore, the new passing point will be 150 yards away.

6. **Economical Progression**

   1, 6, 11, 16, 21, 26. Other solutions are also possible.

7. **Skin and Shoes**

   It is enough to look at only one shoe. If, for example, the white man's right shoe is red, the left one has to be black. This means that the black man will have one left red shoe and one right white shoe, and so on.

8. Up and Down

22 steps. While Zizoloziz goes up the entire staircase, I descend the staircase except for 11 steps (7 at the top + 4 at the bottom). Since he goes twice as fast as I, the entire staircase is 2 x 11 steps.

9. What Month–I

February of a leap year. If a month starts and ends with the same day of the week, it must have a complete number of weeks plus one more day. The only possible month is a 29-day February.

10. What Month–II

August. In order to add up to 38, it can only be the highest possible number for the last Monday of a month (31) and the highest for the first Thursday of a month (7). Therefore, both last month and the current month must have 31 days. The only two 31-day months in a row in the same calendar year are July and August.

11. Eve's Enigma

Thursday. The snake is lying, because it says that today is Saturday and tomorrow is Wednesday. Therefore, today is one of the days when the snake lies (Tuesday, Thursday, and Saturday). It cannot be Saturday or else the snake would not be lying in one statement. Nor can it be Tuesday, for the same reason. It can only be Thursday.

12. Broken M

13. Soccer Scores–I
The Eagles had 5 points. There were ten matches in the tournament with a total of 20 points to be won by the teams. The table already has 15 points assigned. Therefore, the remaining 5 points must belong to the Eagles.

14. Soccer Scores–II
Lions 0, Tigers 0. Lions 1, Bears 0. Tigers 1, Bears 1. The Lions could only win 3 points by winning one match and tying another. Since they only scored one goal, the results must be 1 − 0 and 0 − 0. The Bears tied one and lost the other match. The scores must have been 1 − 1 and 0 − 1. Their tied game must have been against the Tigers. So the Lions beat the Bears 1−0, and the Lions tied the Tigers 0 − 0.

15. What Time Is It–I
5:00. From here, the minute hand will take 30 minutes to reach 6, and the hour hand will take an entire hour.

16. What Time Is It–II
There are two possible times in this situation: 5:15 (the minute hand takes 15 minutes to read 6 and the hour hand takes 45) and 3:45 (the minute hand takes 45 minutes to reach 6 and the hour hand takes 2 hours and 15 minutes, which is 135 minutes).

17. What Time Is It–III
2:12. The hour hand is at the first minute mark after 2, and the minute hand is on the next minute mark.

18. What Time Is It–IV
9:48. The minute hand is on 48 minutes and the hour hand is on the next minute mark.

19. Prohibited Connection (Diagram next page)
Each middle digit (2, 3, 4, and 5) can only be connected to three others (for example, 2 can only be connected to 4, 5, and 6). There are two circles with four connections. We can only put 1 and 6 in them. Once you insert these, the rest is easy to figure out. Another solution exists where the order of the numbers is switched, so 1 and 6 switch, as do 2 and 5, and 3 and 4.

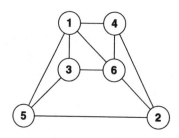

20. Concentric

30 square inches. We turn the small square as shown in the picture. We can see that it is half the size of the big one, as indicated by the dotted lines. These dotted lines divide the large square into eight triangles, and the small square into four triangles.

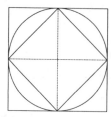

21. John Cash

The reward was 125 dollars. If you erase 1, you have 25 left, which is one-fifth the original amount. If you erase 2, you have 5 left, which is one-fifth of this amount.

To get 125, find a two-digit number in which you can take the first digit off and the result is one-fifth of the number. The only possible number is 25. 25 x 5 = 125.

22. Russian Roulette

The arsenic is in the jar labeled "SUGAR." We know that the snuff is above the salt. They cannot be on the right side, because then the salt would be in the jar labeled "SALT." They cannot be in the center either, because then the second answer would not be true since the coffee and sugar would not be next to each other. Therefore, they are on the left. So the coffee and sugar are in the jars marked "TEA" and "SALT," respectively, leaving arsenic for either the jar marked "ARSENIC" or "SUGAR." Since it's not in the correctly labeled jar, it must be in the jar marked "SUGAR," and the tea is in the jar marked "ARSENIC."

23. New Race

One car goes twice as fast as the other. The first crossing took place at point A. Consider A a new starting point. Do the same for every crossing point. Since they drove at consistent speeds, the distances from A to B, B to C, and C to A are the same. After point A, one car must have driven twice the distance as the other to reach B at the same time. Therefore, one goes twice as fast as the other.

24. The Calculator Keys

There are two possibilities:
1. Change the 4 with the 5 and the 2 with the 8.
$729 - 546 = 183$.
2. Change the 3 with the 9 and the 4 with the 6.
$783 - 654 = 129$.

25. Nice Discounts

You first buy books for $80 and, the next day, for $70, which represents a discount of $70 x .08 = $5.60. (It will be the same result by inverting the order of the purchases, first the $70 purchase and the next day the $80 one.)

26. Enigmatic Fares

98999 and 99000. The tickets are consecutive in number. If the professor had answered "yes" to the question about the five digits of one ticket adding up to 35, the friend could have not figured out the numbers. There would have been several possibilities (78659 and 78660, 36989 and 36990, etc.), so the professor must have answered that indeed none of the tickets added up to 35.

Both tickets add up to 62 (an even number), which means that the first one must end in a 9. If it ended in only one 9, one ticket would add up to 35. Let's call the first ticket ABCD9 and the second one ABC(D + 1)0. The sum is A + B + C + D + 9 + A + B + C + D +

1 = 62, meaning that A + B + C + D + 9 = 35. If it ended in two 9s, the sum of both tickets would give us an odd number. Therefore, the ticket must end in three 9s and no more than three, or the sum wouldn't be 62. We can call the tickets AB999 and A(B + 1)000, where B is not 9. The sum of both is: 2 x (A + B) + 28 = 62. Therefore, A = 9 and B = 8.

27. Horoscope
The teacher is a Pisces. This conversation could have only taken place on February 29. She was 29 then. Six days later (March 6), having turned 30, it becomes true that the date is one fifth of her age. This means her birthday occurs during the six first days of March.

28. Strangers in the Night
The blonde woman killed Mr. Farnanski. There are only four true statements. Only one person is guilty. Therefore, three of the "I'm innocent" statements are true. Only one more statement can be true, and this must be the one made by the man in the dark suit or by the blond woman. Therefore, "The brunette killed him" and "One of the men killed him" are false statements, so the blonde woman is the killer.

29. Monte Carlo
He lost. Every time that Hystrix wins, his money increases 1.5 times (with 100, he bets $50 and if he wins, he has $150). When he loses, his money is reduced by half. So a win-loss combination results in a loss of one quarter of his money. The more he plays, the more money he loses, even though he wins the same number of times as he loses.

30. The Foreigners and the Menu
They could have ordered ABCDD their first night (finding out what D is), AEFGG the second night (finding out what G is and what A is, since they had ordered it the previous night, too), and BEHII the third night (finding out what I, B, and E are). This leaves C, F, and H out, and since they had never ordered these dishes twice and each came on a different night, they should know what they are.

31. Fort Knox Jumping Frogs—I
Move 5 onto 2, 3 onto 7, 1 onto 4, and 6 onto 8.

32. Fort Knox Jumping Frogs—II
Move 5 onto 2, 3 onto 7, 4 onto 13, 6 onto 1, 12 onto 9,
11 onto 14, and 10 onto 8.

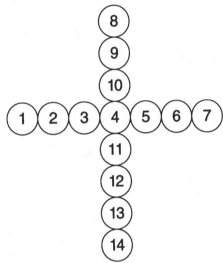

33. Fort Knox Jumping Frogs—III
Move 5 onto 12, 6 onto 4, 10 onto 11, 8 onto 1, 3 onto 2, and
9 onto 7.

34. Fort Knox Jumping Frogs–IV

Move 16 onto 3, 8 onto 5, 17 onto 11, 10 onto 18, 2 onto 15, 7 onto 1, 13 onto 9, 14 onto 20, 12 onto 19, and 6 onto 4.

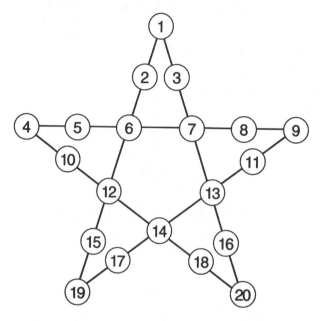

35. Fort Knox Jumping Frogs–V

Move 1 onto 4, 10 onto 7, 11 onto 14, 20 onto 17, 5 onto 3, 6 onto 8, 15 onto 13, 16 onto 18, 2 onto 12, and 19 onto 9.

36. The Harem
There were seven locks. Let's name the locks A, B, C, D, E, F, and G. The vizier had keys for A, B, C, D, E, and F. One of the slaves had the keys for A, B, C, and G. Another one, for A, D, E, and G. Another, for B, D, F, and G. And the last, for C, E, F, and G. With seven locks, the Great Tamerlan's system works–but not with fewer locks.

37. The Dividing End
The number is 381654729.

If the number is ABCDEFGHI, B, D, F, and H are even numbers. The rest are odd numbers. ABCDE can be divided evenly by 5; thus E = 5.

ABCD can be divided evenly by 4. Therefore, CD can also be divided evenly by 4, and since C is an odd number, D can only be 2 or 6.

ABCDEF can be divided evenly by 6 (by 2 and by 3). Since ABC can be divided by 3, DEF can be also. Consequently, DEF is 258 or 654.

You can deduce the rest from here.

38. The Island and the Englishmen
Six Englishmen. Let's draw four circles representing the clubs. Every two clubs have one member in common, so we draw a line from each circle to one point (an Englishman). Each dot is connected to two lines. This is the situation in the illustration, indicating six Englishmen.

39. Logic Apples

Alonso 1, Bertrand 2, George 3, and Kurt 5.
Alonso could not have eaten five or more. Bertrand could not have eaten only one or he would have known that he hadn't eaten more than Alonso. Nor could he have eaten five or more. He could have eaten two, three, or four. George figures this out, although he still doesn't know if he ate more than Bertrand. This means that George must have eaten three or four. Kurt can only deduce the other amounts if he ate five. And the rest, in order to add up to eleven, must have eaten one, two, and three.

40. Added Corners

The 8 cannot be in a corner, so we have to put it in a square. The 7 must go in a square, too. This makes it easy to figure out the rest.

41. Rectangles

Both rectangles have the same area, 40 square inches. If you draw the dotted line you will see that the line divides the inclined figure into two equal pairs of triangles on both sides.

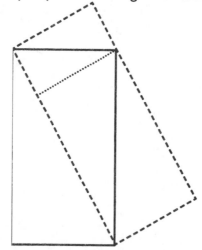

42. A Warm Farewell

10 men and 6 women. The number of handshakes and kisses adds up to 55. Each Porter said good-bye to each Robinson. If we multiply the number of members of both families, the result should be 55. There are two possibilities: $55 = 11 \times 5$ (one family with 11 members and the other one with 5), or $55 = 55 \times 1$ (which could not be possible, since a family is not formed by only one person).

We now analyze the handshakes following the same procedure. There are two possibilities: $21 = 7 \times 3$ (7 men in one family and 3 in the other) or $21 = 21 \times 1$ (which could not be possible, because none of these families has so many members, as seen above). Therefore, one family is formed by 7 men and 4 women, and the other by 3 men and 2 women.

43. Four Minus One Is a Crime

The killer is Mr. A. To go from A to B you will always travel an even number of blocks. However, in the statements there is an odd number (13 blocks from A to the corner of the meeting and from there to B's house). So, either A or B is lying. A similar condition applies to A and C. You will need an odd number of blocks, but the statements talk about an even number. So, either A or C is lying. Therefore, A is lying.

44. On the Route of Marco Polo

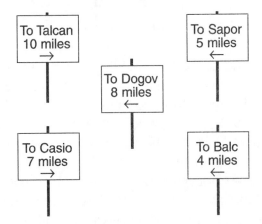

The road signs each point to a different village. The sum of distances in one direction and the sum in the opposite direction must be equal. This can only be achieved with $10 + 7 = 8 + 5 + 4$. Therefore, the signs with 10 and 7 point in one direction and the three others point in the opposite direction.

45. On the Road

10 miles from Philadelphia.

The five signs indicate the following distances: 98, 76, 54, 32, 10.

Other possible sequences include: 90, 81, 72, 63, 54 and 90, 72, 54, 36, 18. However, in all cases the distance from the final sign to Philadelphia is greater.

46. Touching Squares

14 squares.

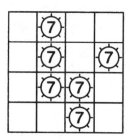

47. Equal Vision

Six watchmen. One way to do it is shown below.

48. Blood and Sand

Lincoln Dustin died at 5:30. At first the commissioner thought that Mr. Dustin had inverted the hourglass at 7:30 (which would account for the 15 hours that the hourglass took to finish). The evident suspect is Begonias, who was at the mansion at the time. Then Begonias told him that he had inverted the hourglass. This made the commissioner think that Mr. Dustin had inverted the hourglass and then Begonias did as well, which means that the time between both inversions counted twice toward the total amount of time. Since the total time was three hours, Begonias inverted the hourglass one and a half hours after Mr. Dustin had. If Begonias said that he had inverted it at 7 p.m., this means that Mr. Dustin inverted it at 5:30.

49. International Summit

A—Spanish, French, Portuguese; B—all; C—all except French; D—Spanish; and E—French and Italian.

Draw a table with five rows and five columns, making the languages the column headers and the people the row headers. Statement 1 tells us that B and C speak English. Mark an X in the corresponding cells. Statement 1 also tells us that D does not speak English. Mark a zero in the corresponding cell. Additionally, Statement 1 tells us B, C, and D speak Spanish. Mark it in the table. Follow the same procedure for Statement 2 and Statement 3. Statement 3 explains that the only common language to C and E is Italian, and since C also speaks English and Spanish, we can write zeroes for E in those columns. In a similar way, write a zero for French in C.

This is how the table will look at this point:

	Eng.	Sp.	Fr.	Port.	Ital.
A			X		
B	X	X	X		
C	X	X	O		X
D	O	X			
E	O	O	X		X

We can see that three people speak Spanish and French. Add another X for Spanish, since it is the most common language. From Statement 6 we need one person who speaks only one language. The only possibility is D. Complete the row with zeroes. From Statement 4 we look for the three people who speak Portuguese. They cannot be C and E, since their common language is Italian. Therefore, two of the Portuguese speakers must be A and B. From Statement 6 we need a person who speaks only two languages. It can only be E, so we write a zero for E in Portuguese. The third person who speaks Portuguese must be C, so we mark an X in the corresponding cell. We look now for the person who speaks three languages, and it can only be A. Fill in the row with zeroes. So, the person who speaks five languages is B. The table is now complete.

50. Mister Digit Face

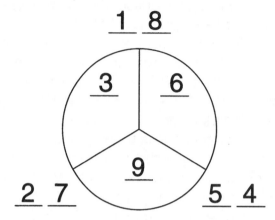

The 9 must be inside the circle, because no product can be 9_ or _9. The 1, 2, and 5 must be outside the circle. From here on you can find the solution. (Other answers can be made by flipping or rotating the circle.)

51. Digit Tree

52. Figures to Cut in Two

53. Segments

| 4 | 7 | 2 | 9 | 1 | 8 | 3 | 6 | 5 |

The numbers 4 and 5 must be at both ends because the sum of the nine digits is 45. Then we place 3 and 6, then 2 and 7, and finally 1, 8, and 9. (The order of the numbers can be reversed.)

54. Multiple Towers

1	→ 9
6	→ 8
9	→ 7
4	→ 6
0	→ 5
2	→ 4
7	→ 3
8	→ 2

5 3

55. Earthlings

Uruguay came in first, Spain second, Zaire third. The second earthling has one answer in common with the first one and one in common with the third one. In which category is the second earthling, then? He cannot always be telling the truth, because he has something in common with a liar, and he cannot always be lying because he has something in common with the honest one. If his first answer were true, then the third one would also be true, and they would be the same as the first and third answers from the honest man. There is no match, however, so this is not the case.

Therefore, the first answer from the man that alternately lies and tells the truth must be a lie. The second is true and the third a lie, so the third man is the honest one, and thus his answers are the results of the soccer championship.

56. The Ant and the Clock

The ant walked 54 minutes. From the first meeting to the second, the minute hand traveled 45 minutes and the ant a distance in minute marks of 105 minutes (45 + a complete 60-minute lap). The illustration below shows the path followed by the ant. The speed ratio is $^{45}/_{105} = {}^{3}/_{7}$. From the start to the first meeting, the minute hand traveled a distance X and the ant (30 − X). Using the speed ratio, this would be $X/(30 − X) = {}^{3}/_{7}$. X = 9 minutes. If we add these to the 45 minutes that it took the ant to get to the second meeting, we come to 54 minutes for the ant's trip.

57. **Hidden Word–I**
VISE

58. **Hidden Word—II**
SOB

59. **Hidden Word–III**
PITHY

60. **Secret Number—I**
3719

61. **Secret Number—II**
9381

62. **Secret Number—III**
2754

63. **Secret Number—IV**
2739

64. **Secret Number—V**
8327

65. **Dominoes Table I**

1	5	5	3	0	6	0	6
5	4	4	2	4	4	6	2
2	6	0	1	1	2	5	1
4	3	5	5	3	2	6	0
0	3	0	3	3	3	1	0
5	2	6	2	3	6	0	1
4	5	6	4	1	4	2	1

66. Dominoes Table II

3	1	2	2	6	1	3	4
5	5	3	4	0	5	3	2
2	6	5	1	1	2	0	0
1	1	0	6	0	3	3	0
0	6	4	3	6	5	4	5
3	2	5	4	0	1	6	2
5	4	6	4	2	4	6	1

67. Dominoes Table III

1	0	2	2	3	6	5
1	6	6	4	3	6	5
2	3	5	0	1	4	6
0	4	3	0	2	4	0
3	6	5	4	5	4	1
0	0	5	1	3	1	2
3	6	2	2	5	3	2
1	1	4	0	4	6	5

68. Dominoes Table IV

5	4	2	3	6	3	4
4	6	5	5	0	6	3
4	6	2	3	4	1	2
6	0	6	3	0	4	1
0	6	0	2	3	4	2
5	5	6	1	4	5	3
5	1	3	2	2	1	1
1	5	2	0	1	0	0

69. Dominoes Table V

4	0	0	1	1	1	0
5	2	3	5	6	5	6
3	5	4	4	3	4	2
2	0	0	5	6	5	3
2	2	1	5	6	0	1
2	4	4	3	2	6	4
5	6	0	3	2	3	6
1	1	3	6	4	1	0

70. Dominoes Table VI

4	5	1	6	0	5	1
2	5	3	5	3	6	5
6	2	0	4	2	2	6
6	6	2	0	5	3	3
3	1	1	2	3	6	4
4	0	3	1	0	0	4
4	1	2	1	4	5	3
5	1	2	0	0	4	6

71. Hound—I

20	13	12	11	⑩
19	14	⑤	6	9
18	⑮	4	7	8
17	16	3	2	1

72. Hound—II

25	26	27	㉘	29	30	31
24	15	⑭	㉟	34	33	32
23	16	13	12	11	8	⑦
22	17	18	1	10	9	6
㉑	20	19	2	3	4	5

162

73. Hound—III

2	1	9	10	11
3	8	16	15	12
4	7	17	14	13
5	6	18	19	20
25	24	23	22	21

74. Hound—IV

25	16	15	12	11
24	17	14	13	10
23	22	21	20	9
2	3	18	19	8
1	4	5	6	7

75. Hound—V

There are two possible solutions.

(13)	12	(11)	8	(7)
14	15	10	9	6
(17)	16	(3)	4	(5)
18	1	(2)	25	24
(19)	20	21	22	(23)

(17)	16	(3)	4	(5)
18	15	(2)	1	6
(19)	14	(13)	12	(7)
20	(23)	24	(11)	8
21	22	25	10	9

76. Poker—I

J	10	J	K	A
8	8	8	A	8
Q	10	A	Q	Q
K	10	K	10	K
A	9	9	9	9

77. Poker—II

9	J	10	Q	K
J	J	Q	Q	Q
A	A	A	A	K
8	J	10	8	K
10	9	10	8	K

78. Poker—III

K	J	K	K	K
9	J	8	Q	10
9	8	J	Q	10
A	J	9	Q	10
A	8	8	A	10

79. Poker—IV

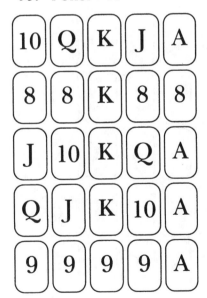

10	Q	K	J	A
8	8	K	8	8
J	10	K	Q	A
Q	J	K	10	A
9	9	9	9	A

80. Poker—V

9	A	9	A	A
8	Q	K	K	10
8	Q	K	J	J
8	A	9	J	10
8	Q	9	J	10

81. Poker—VI

10	Q	Q	Q	10
9	K	J	Q	10
A	K	A	A	A
8	K	J	8	10
J	K	J	8	9

NEARLY IMPOSSIBLE BRAIN BAFFLERS

Are you impossibly smart? If you answer all of these tricky number, word, chess, logic, and spatial puzzles, you must be!

Along the way you'll try to decipher a Top Forty song chart, decide whether you'd rather a tiger chase you or a zebra, and give three boys' names that are anagrams of one another.

Fortunately, the answers are provided—but don't look unless you must!

The answers for this section can be found on pages 222 through 247.

1

What word, expression, or name is depicted below?

FAREDCE

2

Find a ten-digit number containing each digit once, so that the number formed by the first n digits is divisible by n for each value of n between 1 and 10.

3

When the examination results were published, one college found that all 32 of its students were successful in at least one of the three exams that each of them had taken. Of the students who did not pass Exam One, the number who passed Exam Two was exactly half of the number who passed Exam Three. The number who passed only Exam One was the same as the number who passed only one of the other two exams, and three more than the number who passed Exam One and at least one of the other two exams.

How many students passed more than one exam?

4

If 89 players enter a single elimination tennis tournament, how many matches would it take to decide the winner, excluding byes?

5

Using exactly two 2s and any of the standard mathematical symbols, write down an expression whose value is five.

6

What word, expression, or name is depicted below?

7

This puzzle was devised by Dr. Karl Fabel and published in 1949 in "T.R.D.'s Diamond Jubilee" issue of the *Fairy Chess Review*.

White to play and mate in sixty.

8

What word, expression, or name is depicted below?

T RN

9

Find a ten-digit number whose first digit is the number of 1s in the number, whose second digit is the number of 2s in the number, whose third digit is the number of 3s in the number, and so on up to the tenth digit, which is the number of 0s in the number.

10

Without using a calculator, guess which is bigger: e^π or π^e?

11

A selection of eight cards is dealt with every second card being returned to the bottom of the pack. Thus the top card goes to the table, card two goes to the bottom of the pack, card three goes to the table, card four to the bottom of the pack, and so on. This procedure continues until all the cards are dealt.

The order in which the cards appear on the table is:

A K A K A K A K

How were the cards originally stacked?

12

Gambler A chooses a series of three possible outcomes from successive throws of a die, depending simply on whether the number thrown each time is odd (O) or even (E). Gambler B then chooses a different series of three successive possible outcomes. The die is then thrown as often as necessary until either gambler's chosen series of outcomes occurs.

For example, Gambler A might choose the series EOE and B might choose OEE. If successive throws gave, say, EEOOEOE, then A would win the game after the seventh throw. Had the sixth throw been E rather than O, then B would have won.

A has chosen the series EEE and B, who was thinking of choosing OEE, changes his mind to OOO. Has B reduced his chance of winning the game or is it still the same?

13

What word, expression, or name is depicted below?

```
RI
D   N
 S K
HOUSE
```

14

Find three different two-digit primes where the average of any two is a prime, and the average of all three is a prime.

15

Each letter in the sum below represents a different digit. Can you crack the code and discover the uncoded sum?

```
    T  W  E  L  V  E
    T  W  E  L  V  E
    T  W  E  L  V  E
    T  W  E  L  V  E
    T  W  E  L  V  E
 +  T  H  I  R  T  Y
 ─────────────────────
    N  I  N  E  T  Y
```

16

A spider is in a rectangular warehouse measuring 40 x 10 x 10 meters. The spider is on the 10 x 10–meter wall, five meters from the sides and one meter above the ground. The proverbial fly is on the opposite wall, five meters from the sides and one meter below the ceiling. What is the shortest route for the spider to walk to the fly?

17

What word, expression, or name is depicted below?

18

In a game of table tennis, 24 of the 37 points played were won by the player serving, and Smith beat Jones 21 – 16. Remembering in table tennis that service alternates every 5 points, who served first?

19

This chess puzzle by C.S. Kipping was published in the *Manchester City News* in 1911.

White to play and mate in three.

20

What word, expression, or name is depicted below?

EVER
EVER
EVER
EVER
EVER

21

In the three envelopes shown, all the envelopes have one statement that is true and one that is false.

1

1. The formula is not in here.
2. The formula is not in Envelope 3.

2

3. The formula is in Envelope 2.
4. The formula is not in Envelope 1.

3

5. The formula is not in here.
6. The formula is not in Envelope 1.

Which envelope contains the formula?

22

How can eleven matches make nine, nine matches make ten, and ten matches make five?

23

Caesar and Brutus are playing a game in which each says the next number from a well-known sequence. The first 20 terms of the sequence are given below:

1 2 3 2 1 2 3 4 2 1 2 3 4 3 2 3 4 5 3 2

The fortieth term is 2. If Caesar began the game, who will be the first to say "10"?

24

This (okay, somewhat misshapen) Valentine heart consists of one large semicircle beneath two smaller semicircles. The arrow passes right through the point at which the two smaller semicircles meet.

Which part of the heart's perimeter is the longer: that lying above the line of the arrow, or that lying below?

25

What word, expression, or name is depicted below?

BEND
DRAW
DRAW
DRAW

This week's chart of the top 40 pop songs has just been published. The song that was at number 35 in last week's chart has dropped out, and there is a new entry at number 32. There are also five non-movers, at positions 1, 23, 29, 31, and 37. Of the other 34 songs in the new chart, 18 have moved up and 16 down, but in every instance the number of positions moved, whether up or down, was a factor (greater than one, but possibly equal to the number itself) of the song's position in last week's chart.

The titles of last week's top 40 are shown below. Complete this week's chart.

Last week		This week	Last week		This week
Atomic	1	Atomic	Valentine	21	
Blockbuster	2		What	22	
Classic	3		Xanadu	23	Xanadu
Dizzy	4		YMCA	24	
Emma	5		Zabadak!	25	
Footloose	6		Autumn Almanac	26	
Gaye	7		Angie Baby	27	
Hello	8		Another Day	28	
Intuition	9		Angel Eyes	29	Angel Eyes
Jesamine	10		Angel Fingers	30	
Kayleigh	11		Amateur Hour	31	Amateur Hour
Lamplight	12		Angela Jones	32	New entry
Mickey	13		Ain't Nobody	33	
Night	14		American Pie	34	
Obsession	15		Ant Rap	35	
Perfect	16		Alphabet Street	36	
Question	17		Alternate Title	37	Alternate Title
Reward	18		As Usual	38	
Sandy	19		Adoration Waltz	39	
True	20		Always Yours	40	

27

What word, expression, or name is depicted below?

agb

28

The following was originally a list of five-letter words, but in each case two consecutive letters (though never the first two) have been removed. The 26 missing letters are all different. What was the original list?

A	N	T
A	S	S
B	A	Y
C	O	Y
D	I	M
E	E	L
F	A	R
M	A	R
P	I	E
S	E	E
T	I	E
T	O	P
W	I	N

29

There is one in a minute and two in a moment, but only one in a million years. What are we talking about?

30

Find nine different integers from 1 to 20 inclusive such that no combination of any three of the nine integers forms an arithmetic progression. For example, if two of the integers chosen were 7 and 13, then that would preclude 1, 10, and 19 from being included.

31

This puzzle was composed by Hans August and Dr. Karl Fabel, and was published in 1949 in **Romana de Sah**.

White has just made his seventeenth move. What was Black's ninth move, and what were the moves that followed it?

32

Two travelers set out at the same time to travel opposite ways round a circular railway. Trains start each way every 15 minutes, on the hour, 15 minutes past, half past, and 45 minutes past. Clockwise trains take two hours for the journey, and counterclockwise trains take three hours. Including trains seen at the starting point and the ones they are traveling on, how many trains did each traveler see on his journey?

33

The Roman numerals that are still used are I = 1, V = 5, X = 10, L = 50, C = 100, D = 500, and M = 1000. Examples of four Roman numbers are VIII = 8, LXXVI = 76, CXXXVI = 136, and MDCCCLXII = 1862.

Today, the Roman numbers IIII, VIIII, and DCCCC are usually abbreviated as IV, IX, and CM, respectively, a numeral to the left of a higher numeral denoting subtraction. Where there is an opportunity, these abbreviations are used in this cross-number, together with CD for CCCC, XC for LXXXX, and XL for XXXX. Thus 1904 would be written as MCMIV and 49 as XLIX. Note that the logical extension of this method of abbreviation, such as IL for 49, for example, was never fully developed and so is not used here. All that is used, where there is an opportunity, are the six usual abbreviations already mentioned.

In the grid below all answers are Roman numerals and, when converted to Arabic (normal) numbers, are palindromes (none starting with zero) of two digits or more. One number occurs twice; the rest are all different.

34

We place in a box 13 white marbles and 15 black. We also have 28 black marbles outside the box.

We remove two marbles from the box. If they have a different color, we put the white one back in the box. If they have the same color, we put a black marble in the box. We continue doing this until only one marble is left in the box. What is its color?

35

What word, expression, or name is depicted below?

at
the
•
of
on

36

A drawer contains a number of red and blue socks. If I pull two out at random, then the chance of their being a red pair is a half and the chance of their being a blue pair is a twelfth. How many socks are in the drawer?

37

A long time ago, you could buy eight hens for a dollar or one sheep for a dollar, and cows were ten dollars each. A farmer buying animals of each type bought a hundred animals for a hundred dollars.
What animals did he buy?

38

Are 1997 nickels worth more than 1992 nickels?

39

What word, expression, or name is depicted below?

40

Insert the missing letter:

J ? M A M J J A

41

In a league of four soccer teams, each team played the other three teams. 2 points were awarded for a win and 1 point for a tie. After all six games were played, a final league table was prepared, as shown below:

Team	Won	Tied	Lost	Goals for	Goals against	Points
A	3	0	0	6	1	6
B	1	1	1	2	4	3
C	1	0	2	2	2	2
D	0	1	2	2	5	1

What was the score in each of the six games?

42

Lynsey is a biology student. Her project for this term is measuring the effect of an increase in vitamin C in the diet of 25 laboratory mice. Each mouse will have a different diet supplement of between 1 and 50 units. Fractions of a unit are not possible.

Although the university pays for the mouse food, Lynsey has to buy the vitamin C supplement herself. The first consideration in designing this experiment was therefore to minimize the total number of supplements.

The second consideration was that no mouse should have an exact multiple of another mouse's supplement. Thus, if one mouse was on a supplement of 14 units, then this would preclude supplements of 1, 2, 7, 28, and 42 units.

What supplements should Lynsey use?

43

Find two ten-digit numbers, each containing the digits from 0 to 9 once and once only, with the property that successive pairs of digits, from left to right, are divisible in turn by 2, 3, 4, 5, 6, 7, 8, 9, and 10.

44

What word, expression, or name is depicted below?

STEP
PETS
PETS

45

What are the numbers in the tenth line of the following pyramid?

1
11
21
1211
111221
312211
13112221
1113213211
31131211131221

46

What word, expression, or name is depicted below?

READING

47

What digit does each letter represent in the multiplication below, given that no two letters stand for the same digit?

LAGER
x 4
REGAL

48

The order of the clues has been muddled up, but 21-Across is correct.

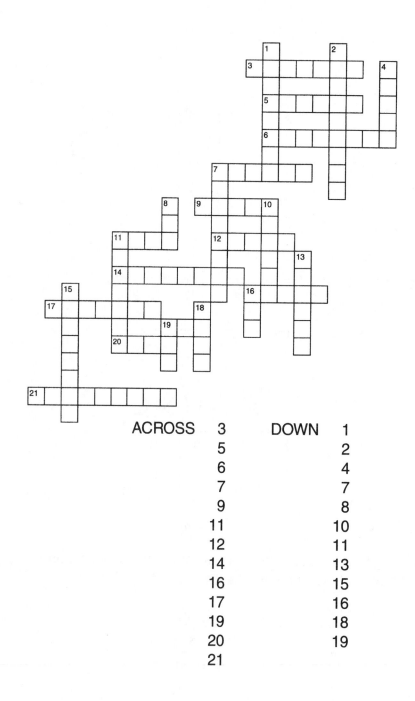

ACROSS	3	DOWN	1
	5		2
	6		4
	7		7
	9		8
	11		10
	12		11
	14		13
	16		15
	17		16
	19		18
	20		19
	21		

What word, expression, or name is depicted below?

B
A E
D U M R

50

Letters other than "x" each represent a different digit. An "x", however, may represent any digit. There is no remainder. Find which digits the letters and each "x" stand for:

```
                      O N E
   T R Y / T H I S x
           x x x
             x x x
             x x x
             x x x x
             x x x x
```

51

The number 6 has factors (not counting itself) of 1, 2, and 3, which add up to 6. The number 28 has the same property, since its factors, 1, 2, 4, 7, and 14, add up to 28. What four-digit number has this property?

52

Between noon and midnight, but not counting these times, how often will the minute hand and hour hand of a clock overlap?

53

What word, expression, or name is depicted below?

54

A set of building blocks contains a number of wooden cubes. The six faces of each cube are painted, each with a single color, in such a way that no two adjacent faces have the same color. Given that only five different colors have been used and that no two of the blocks are identical in their colorings, what is the maximum number of blocks there can be in the set?

55

The Bowls Club has fewer than 100 members. To the nearest whole number, 28% of the members are former committee members, 29% are current committee members, and 42% have never been on the committee. Again to the nearest whole number, 35% of the former committee members are women. What is the total membership of the club?

56

The pars for a nine-hole golf course designed by a mathematician are:

3 3 5 4 4 3 5 5 4

On which very well known series (as well known as one, two, three, etc.) are the pars based?

57

This may seem self-contradictory, but find three integers in arithmetic progression (that is, with equal differences, such as 230, 236, and 242) whose product is prime.

58

What is the next term in this series:

1248 1632 6412 8256 ?

59

What word, expression, or name is depicted below?

ONE
T
S

60

The ages of Old and Young total 48. Old is twice as old as Young was when Old was half as old as Young will be when Young is three times as old as Old was when Old was three times as old as Young.
How old is Old?

61

Consider a 5 x 5 version of a chessboard with one player having five queens and the other player three queens. There are no other pieces. Can you place the queens on the board so that neither player's queens can capture one of his or her opponent's queens?

62

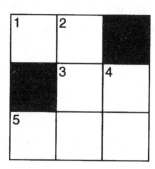

ACROSS
1. Starting piece between 3 and 4
3. 2-Down minus a perfect square
5. Three!

DOWN
2. A perfect square
4. 1.5 times 5-Across (or ⅔ of 5-Across)

63

What word, expression, or name is depicted below?

NE14
10S?

64

A full set of dominoes (0-0 to 6-6) has been laid out in a rectangular array. The numbers in the diagram represent the spots on the dominoes, and the puzzle is to identify the position of each domino within the pattern.

```
1 2 6 1 6 3 4 5
3 3 6 4 3 2 5 4
3 0 6 0 3 1 2 2
0 5 5 4 6 5 0 2
0 2 5 1 5 0 0 1
6 4 3 4 4 1 1 1
2 2 6 4 5 0 3 6
```

65

At the end of the soccer season, every player had scored a prime number of goals and the average for the eleven players was also a prime number. No player's tally was the same as anyone else's, and neither was it the same as the average.

Given that nobody had scored more than 45 goals, how many goals did each player score?

66

What word, expression, or name is depicted below?

timing

tim   ing

67

Allwyn, Aitkins, and Arthur are to fight a three-way duel. The order in which they shoot will be determined by lot and they will continue to shoot until two are dead. Allwyn never misses, Aitkins is 80% accurate, and Arthur, the cleverest of the three, hits his target just half of the time. Who has the best chance of surviving?

68

What word, expression, or name is depicted below?

GR12"AVE

69

Can you subdivide a square measuring 11 x 11 into five rectangles such that the five lengths and five widths of the rectangles are all different and integral? There are two solutions.

70

What are the missing numbers?

31   62   __   25   56   __   19

71

Find three different positive integers whose factorials are each one less than a perfect square, and whose factorials sum to a perfect square.

72

I recently overheard a conversation that went roughly as follows:

Bob: "Here's a problem that might interest you. On my bus this morning there were only three other passengers, all of whom I knew. We discovered that the product of their ages was 2,450, and that the sum was exactly twice your age. How old are they?"

Jim: "Hang on. You haven't given me enough info."

Bob: "Oh, sorry. I forgot to mention that one of the passengers on the bus was someone older than me, and I am—"

Jim: "I know how old you are. And I now know the passengers' ages, too."

How old are Jim, Bob, and each of the three other passengers?

73

This puzzle is based on a theme by W.A. Shinkman, and the mate-in-three was first solved by Sam Loyd. The puzzle below was published in the *Leeds Mercury Supplement* in 1895.

White to play and mate in three.

74

Construct a game that will leave the position shown for Puzzle 73 after Black's sixteenth move.

75

In a game of poker, one of the hands of five cards had the following features:

- There was no card above a 10 (an ace is above a 10 in poker).
- No two cards were of the same value.
- All four suits were represented.
- The total values of the odd and even cards were equal.
- No three cards were in sequence.
- The black cards totaled 10 in value.
- The hearts totaled 14.
- The lowest card was a spade.

What was the hand?

76

What word, expression, or name is depicted below?

```
D    d    D
d    W    d
D    d    D
```

77

"Bookkeeper" has three consecutive double letters. What common two-word phrase, if you remove the space, also has three consecutive double letters?

78

What word, expression, or name is depicted below?

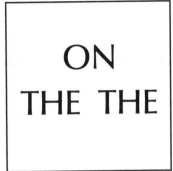

ON

THE THE

79

Divide the following figure into four identical parts, with each part made up of whole squares only. Each of the four parts should also contain one O and one X, but not necessarily in the same relative positions.

O			X		
			X		
		O			
	X		X		
			O	O	

80

Using each of the numbers 1, 5, 6, and 7 once and once only, parentheses as required, and any combination and any number of the following symbols: + − x /, find an expression that equals 21.

81

P and Q are integers that between them contain each of the digits from 0 to 9 once and once only. What is the maximum value of P x Q?

82

What word, expression, or name is depicted below?

COTAXME

83

A total of five triangles can be seen in the diagram on the left.

How many triangles can be found in the diagram on the right?

84

Both my father and my father's grandfather were born in years that can be expressed as $m^n - n^m$, where m and n are both integers.
In which years were they born?

85

What word, expression, or name is depicted below?

86

In this long division, each "x" represents a digit. Find which digits each "x" stands for:

```
                              x   x . x   x   x
              x   x / x   x   x   x
                      x   x
                      x   x   x
                        x   x
                        x   x
                        x   x
                        x   x   x
                        x   x   x
                            x   x
                            x   x
```

87

What are the two missing numbers in the series below?

_ _ 3 3 7 7 2 3 6 5

88

Five soccer teams, United, County, Rovers, Albion, and Thistle, took part in a league tournament. Their colors were white, yellow, green, red, and blue, though not necessarily in that order. No teams were tied in the standings at the end of the tournament. From the following information, determine for each team its captain, colors, and position in which it finished in the league.

• Rovers did not win the league, but finished higher than fourth.
• Neither Albion nor the team in green finished in the top three.
• Evans captained the team in yellow.
• Cooke's team finished ahead of County, which was captained by Dixon.
• Allen's team finished second and Boyle's team finished last.
• The team in white finished lower than both United and the team in blue, but above Evans's team.
• Albion was not the green team and United was not the blue team.

89

What word, expression, or name is depicted below?

Symphon

90

Arrange the digits from 1 to 9 in a 3 x 3 array in such a way that the sum of a number's immediate neighbors (including diagonals) is a multiple of that number.

9	5	1
6	7	2
4	3	8

The example shows an unsatisfactory attempt. The three numbers bordering 9 add to 18, which is a multiple of 9 as required, and the numbers bordering 1, 2, 3, 4, and 5 also meet the condition specified. The numbers bordering 6, 7, and 8, however, do not meet the required condition.

91

What word, expression, or name is depicted below?

GIVE GET
GIVE GET
GIVE GET
GIVE GET

92

What is the minimum difference between two integers that between them contain each digit once?

93

This position was created by F. Amelung and published in ***Düna Zeitung*** in 1897. It is a puzzle that has since defeated many good chess players, and one cannot but wonder whether it has ever occurred naturally in a real game. If it did, and you were White and about to play, how could you force mate in two?

White to play and mate in two.

94

Arrange the digits from one to nine in a 3 x 3 square in such a way that each of the three-digit numbers reading across, and the three-digit number on the diagonal from top left to bottom right, are all perfect squares.

95

The digital root of a number is obtained by summing its digits and then repeating this process until the answer is a single digit. For example, the digital root of 8777 is 2.

Noting that any number divisible by nine has a digital root of nine, what is the digital root of $(9^{6130} + 2)^{4875}$?

96

If six equilateral triangles, each of one unit in area, are joined edge to edge, twelve different shapes each of six units in area can be constructed as shown below:

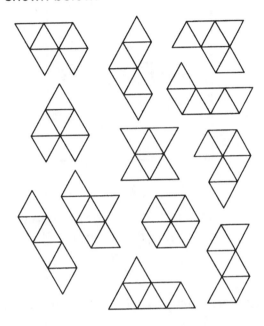

Show that it is impossible to form any six of these shapes into a 6 x 6 x 6 equilateral triangle of 36 units in area.

97

Which of the following poker hands is stronger?

A♣ A♦ A♥ K♣ K♥ or A♣ A♥ K♣ K♦ K♠

Think about it!

98

Continue the sequence:

202 122 232 425 262 728 ? ?

99

What word, expression, or name is depicted below?

VAD ERS

100

The third and fourth powers of this integer contain between them exactly one of each digit. What is the integer?

101

Complete the eight words using each letter of the alphabet once and once only.

```
_ A _ E R I _ _
_ U _ _ _ E
_ I _ E
_ _ L _ E R
_ I _ _
_ _ A P
B R _ _ _ N
_ O L _ _ A _
```

102

Is the tenth root of ten
A little bit more
Than the root of the square
Of the sixth root of four?

103

This cross-number uses Roman numerals only and yes, every clue is the same! If you are struggling to remember what the Roman numerals are and how they are used, a description is given in Puzzle 33 on page 179.

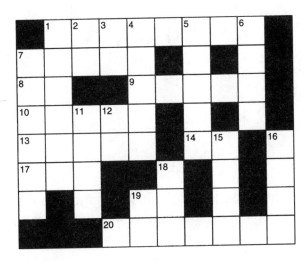

ACROSS

1 A perfect square
7 A perfect square
8 A perfect square
9 A perfect square
10 A perfect square
13 A perfect square
14 A perfect square
17 A perfect square
19 A perfect square
20 A perfect square

DOWN

1 A perfect square
2 A perfect square
3 A perfect square
4 A perfect square
5 A perfect square
6 A perfect square
7 A perfect square
11 A perfect square
12 A perfect square
15 A perfect square
16 A perfect square
18 A perfect square
19 A perfect square

104

What word, expression, or name is depicted below?

DNA4TH

105

A horizontal line from the top of the inside edge of a bicycle tire to the two outside edges of the tire measures 24 centimeters as shown in the side view below:

24 cm

What is the area of the bicycle tire visible from this view?

106

In the following line, cross out six letters so that the remaining letters, without altering their sequence, will spell a familiar English word.

B S A I N X L E A T N T E A R S

107

What word, expression, or name is depicted below?

ping**WILLOW**

108

What is the smallest integer that can be expressed as the sum of two squares in three different ways? The answer is less than 500.

109

Two right triangles share the same hypotenuse AB. The shorter sides of the first triangle are 13 and 18 units; the shorter sides of the second are 7 and 20 units.

Clearly we are not measuring in base ten. What base is being used, and how long is the hypotenuse?

110

A ball with a diameter of 40 centimeters is lying on the ground, tight against a wall:

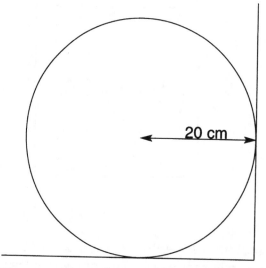

20 cm

Can a ball with a diameter of seven centimeters pass through the gap between the ball, ground, and wall?

111

What word, expression, or name is depicted below?

1 D   5 U
2 R   6 L
3 A   7 A
4 C

112

What word, expression, or name is depicted below?

wear

long

113

This puzzle by Sam Loyd was published in the *Holyoke Transcript* in 1876.

White to play and mate in three.

114

"Strength" is an eight-letter word with only one vowel. What's an eight-letter word with five vowels in a row?

115

The array of blocks shown below spells the word "PUZZLE." Could we be looking at six different views of the same block, or is one or more of the views inconsistent with the others?

116

What word, expression, or name is depicted below?

117

Using the digits 1 to 9 in ascending order and no more than three standard arithmetical signs, find an expression that equals 100. An example that uses six standard arithmetical signs is shown below:

$$1 + (2 \times 3) - 4 + (56 \div 7) + 89 = 100$$

118

If the integers that contain each digit once were arranged in ascending order, which would be the millionth? (Numbers can't start with 0.)

119

A Christmas decoration comprises a symmetrical four-pointed star supported by three threads. The decoration hangs in the center of a small circular window:

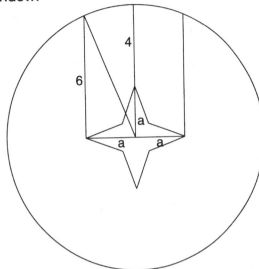

The central thread is four centimeters long, and the outer two are each six centimeters long. What is the width of the star?

120

What word, expression, or name is depicted below?

79 S 34 A 92
F 185 E 376
7 T 27 Y 12

121

One for the children: Would you rather a tiger chased you or a zebra?

122

In the expression below, do the three letters represent three different digits?

$$(ANNE)_{base\ 8} - (ANNE)_{base\ 5} = (ANNE)_{base\ 7}$$

123

Eric the Halibut is swimming to the right. Move three sticks (and his eye, smile, and bubbles) so that he is swimming to the left.

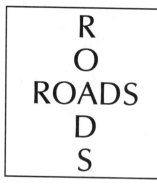

124

What word, expression, or name is depicted below?

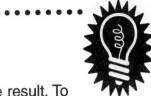

125

Losers' Chess is a fun game that often turns in a surprise result. To play it, ignore checks and checkmates, for the object is either to lose all of one's men, king included, or be stalemated (unable to play a move). Players must capture an opponent's man if they can, but where there is a choice, can choose which. All other rules are the same as for ordinary chess.

Puzzles in Losers' Chess are rare, and ones with an unusual twist like the one below even rarer. This one, by T.R. Dawson, was first published in 1925 in **Das Wochenschach**. In the first analysis it looks like Black can force White to stalemate him, but White, who is playing up the board, can play and win by forcing Black to cause the stalemate. How?

White to play and win (Losers' Chess rules).

126

A ladder five meters long leans against a wall. A box measuring 1 x 1 x 1 meters just fits in the gap. If the base of the ladder is nearer to the wall than the top of the ladder is to the ground, how far is the base of the ladder from the wall?

127

No answer begins with a zero.

ACROSS

1 See 3-Down
3 A multiple of 3
8 3 x 17-Down
9 2 x 15-Down
10 See 14-Down
11 See 6-Down
13 2 x 4-Down
16 Not 3-Down
18 See 5-Down
20 2 x 2-Down
21 Not 6-Down
22 See 1-Down
23 Same as 20-Down

DOWN

1 2 x 22-Across
2 See 20-Across
3 2 x 1-Across
4 See 13-Across
5 2 x 18-Across
6 3 x 11-Across
7 Same as 23-Across
12 2 x 3-Across
14 2 x 10-Across + 4
15 See 9-Across
17 See 8-Across
19 Square of 23-Across
20 See 23-Across

128

What number, when spelled out, has no repeated letters and has each of the vowels (not including Y) once?

129

What word, expression, or name is depicted below?

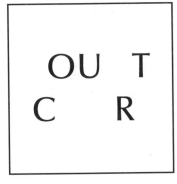

OU   T
C   R

130

Shown below are six numbered pool balls arranged in a triangular pattern such that each number in the pattern is equal to the difference between the two numbers above:

4 1 6
3 5
2

Find a similar triangular pattern for fifteen pool balls numbered 1 to 15.

131

What is the next term in this series?

100 121 144 202 244 400 ____

132

What are the next two letters in the following series and why?

W A T N T L I T F S _ _

133

The diagram shows a regular pentagram:

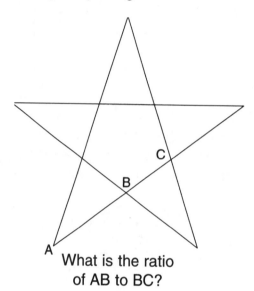

What is the ratio
of AB to BC?

134

If B is two A,
C three A plus B,
And A is "eleven eleven,"
Is B to the C
Plus C to the B
Divisible by seven?

"Eleven eleven,"
So you won't be confused,
Has nothing to do with odd bases.
It's simply ten thou
That's multiplied by
One ninth to four decimal places.

135

Reconstruct the following multiplication, using the digits 2, 3, 5, and 7 only.

```
        x   x   x
            x   x
    ─────────────
    x   x   x   x
x   x   x   x
────────────────
x   x   x   x   x
```

136

What word, expression, or name is depicted below?

FEWFEW
MENTION
MENTION

137

Find a three-digit number containing three different digits where the first digit plus the number formed by the second and third digits, the first digit multiplied by the number formed by the second and third digits, and the sum of the three digits are all perfect squares.

138

Which three boys' names are anagrams of one another?

139

Five checks by White in four moves (including a double check) followed by a checkmate to solve a puzzle that is more than 500 years old! It was first published by Lucena in 1496.

White to play and mate in five.

140

Two equal squares, ABCD and DEFG, have the vertex D in common. The angle between the two squares is 60 degrees:

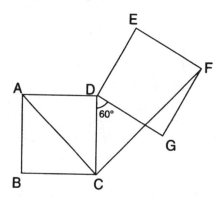

What is the angle ACF?

141

Heather left her hotel room between 7 and 8 p.m. and glanced at her watch. When she next looked at her watch it appeared as if the hour and minute hands had changed places. In fact, it was now between 10 and 11 p.m. Exactly how long ago had she left her room?

142

What word, expression, or name is depicted below?

143

Find a four-digit number, with four different digits, that is equal to the number formed by its digits in descending order minus the number formed by its digits in ascending order.

144

Two candles, one of which was two centimeters longer than the other, were lit for Halloween. The longer and thinner one was lit at 4 p.m. and the shorter but fatter one fifteen minutes later. Each candle burned at a steady rate, and by 8 p.m. both were the same length. The thinner one finally burned out at midnight and the fatter one an hour later. How long was each candle originally?

145

What word, expression, or name is depicted below?

PR^{house}AIRIE

PR͟house͟AIRIE

146

The following eight numbers can be grouped into four pairs such that the higher of each pair divided by the lower is a number (to an average of five decimal places) of particular mathematical significance.

113 323 355 408 577 610 878 987

What are the four pairs?

147

The following relationships hold among the ages of the members of a family of four. All ages are integral.

The mother is three times as old as the daughter was when the father was the same age as the mother is now. When the daughter reaches half the age the mother is now, the son will be half as old as the father was when the mother was twice the age the daughter is now. When the father reaches twice the age the mother was when the daughter was the same age as the son is now, the daughter will be four times as old as the son is now. Given that one of their ages is a perfect square, what are the four ages?

148

What word, expression, or name is depicted below?

LE
VEL

149

Find a 3 x 3 magic square in which the following properties are true:
- The sum of each row, column, and long diagonal is 111.
- Each cell has a number with no factors other than one and itself.
- Each cell is different.
  As a hint, you should start by figuring out the center square.

150

Twice eight are ten of us, and ten but three.
Three of us are five. What can we be?
If this is not enough, I'll tell you more.
Twelve of us are six, and nine but four.

151

In the expression below, each letter represents a different digit:

$$A^5 + B^5 + C^5 + D^5 + E^5 = ABCDE$$

What is ABCDE?

152

This self-mate in four was first published by William Shinkman in the *Chess Player's Chronicle* in 1883.

In a fit of kindness, White decides she wants Black to win and offers her resignation. Black turns down White's offer by announcing that he thinks the game should be played to the finish.

White then forced Black to mate her in four moves anyway.
How does White do this?

153

What word, expression, or name is depicted below?

154

A professor asked four students how long each of them had been studying. One of the students replied: "We have all been studying a whole number of years, the sum of our years of studying is equal to the number of years you have been teaching, and the product of our years of studying is 180."

"I'm sorry," replied the professor after some thought, "but that doesn't give me enough information."

"Yes, you're right," agreed another of the students. "But if we told you whether any of us were into double figures in our years of study, then you could answer your question."

How long had each of the four been studying?

155

In how many different ways can the 16 chess pieces be arranged on one side of a chessboard for the start of a game of chess? For example, the two rooks can switch places, and any two of the eight pawns can be swapped and still leave the standard starting position.

156

What word, expression, or name is depicted below?

Lu cky

157

In an athletics contest between the army, the navy, and the air force, each team entered three athletes in a particular race. The winning athlete scored 8 points, the runner-up 7, third place 6, and so on down to none for last place.

Once the race was run, the judges needed a photograph to separate the first two army men to finish. A member of the navy's team finished last. When the points were totaled, all three teams were found to have the same score.

Find by team the order in which the nine athletes finished.

158

What word, expression, or name is depicted below?

159

In a game of chess, Black has agreed to mirror White's first three moves. White promptly mates Black on the fourth move. What were White's moves?

160

Which day of the week has an anagram?

161

What word, expression, or name is depicted below?

OWHER

162

What word, expression, or name is depicted below?

HOROBOD

Answers

1. Red in the face.

2. 3,816,547,290.

3. Eleven students passed Exam One only, three passed Exam Two only, and eight passed Exam Three only. Thus ten students passed more than one exam.

4. Each match will eliminate one player, so starting with 89 players will require 88 matches to decide the winner.

5. $\sqrt{.2}^{-2}$, which shows that two 2s can make five!

6. Square meal.

7. For White to win, he has to force one of Black's knights to move.

   Then, provided White's king is safe from unwanted checks and White has not moved his own knights, White wins with Ne4 mate or Nd5 mate. The actual winning move will depend upon which knight Black eventually moves.

   Black can delay moving a knight for 59 moves! His tactic is to shunt the rook at a4 to and fro to a3 whenever he can. Accordingly, and taking the route that avoids unwanted checks, White uses his king to inhibit the shunting rook by timing the arrival of his king at b5 to follow Black's move Ra3.

   On the first four occasions White does this, Black keeps his rook out of danger by moving a pawn on the e file. On the fifth occasion, to avoid moving a knight and to save his rook, Black must block his rook in with a5–a4. On his next move Black is compelled to move a knight and expose himself to an instant checkmate. Note that if Black moves his pawns before he has to, then the mate is simply speeded up. With Black's best defense as shown below, White will mate in sixty.

   White's first move can be either Ke8 or Kd6. White's king then proceeds d7, c8, b7, b6, b5. By moving to d7 via e8 or d6, the White king arrives at b5 after an even number of moves. Thus, for move six, Black's shunting rook will be at a3 and Black must move a pawn, lose his rook, or be mated. To defer mate as long as possible, Black must play e4–e3.

After Black's move, e4–e3, White moves his king away from b5 and Black can continue with the shunting of his rook. White must now move his king back to b5 in an odd number of moves in order to catch the shunting rook at a3. The shortest route for White to achieve this that avoids unwanted checks is b6, b7, c8, d7, e8, f8, f7, e8, d7, c8, b7, b6, b5, and this he repeats four times. On moves 19, 32, and 45 Black takes a break from shunting his rook and moves a pawn on the e file. On move 58, however, Black can do no better than to block his rook in with a5–a4. White then plays a waiting move, Kb6. If Black moves the knight at b4, then White mates with Nd5, and if Black moves the knight at d2, then White mates with Ne4. This gives White mate in sixty.

8. No U-Turn.

9. 2,100,010,006.

10. e^{π} is greater than π^{e}. To two decimal places, $e^{\pi} = 23.14$ and $\pi^{e} = 22.46$.

11. AAKAAKKK.

12. By changing his mind, B reduced his chance of winning the game.

The only way in which EEE can appear before OEE is if the first three throws of the die are EEE. Otherwise the sequence EEE must be preceded by an O. The probability of the first three throws being E is $(\frac{1}{2})^{3}$, so if B chooses OEE when A has chosen EEE, then B wins with probability $\frac{7}{8}$. If B chooses OOO in response to A's choice of EEE, then B's chance of winning is $\frac{1}{2}$.

13. Round of drinks on the house.

14. 11, 47, and 71.

15. TWELVE = 130760, THIRTY = 194215, and NINETY = 848015.

16. A straight-line route that takes the spider one meter down to the floor, forty meters across the floor, and nine meters up toward the ceiling is fifty meters.

Two quicker straight-line routes, found by drawing straight lines from the spider to the fly on a flattened plan of the warehouse, are shown below. The first of these sees the spider heading up the side wall, crossing the ceiling, and finally approaching the fly from above. The distance of this route is $\sqrt{(14^2 + 46^2)} = 48.08$ meters.

The third straight-line route sees the spider heading diagonally to the floor, then up the side wall, crossing the corner of the ceiling and again at the end approaching the fly from above. The distance of this route is $\sqrt{(20^2 + 42^2)} = 46.52$ meters.

The shortest route is 46.52 meters.

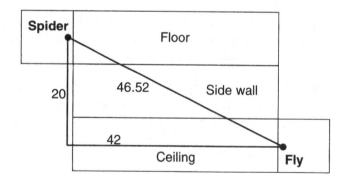

17. Ambiguous.

18. Smith served first. One possible proof is as follows:
Whoever served first would have served on 20 of the points played and the other player would have served on 17 of them. Suppose the first player won x of the points on which he served

and y of the points served by his opponent. The total number of points lost by the player who served them is then 20 − x + y. This must equal 13, since we are told that 24 of the 37 points were won by the player serving. Thus x = 7 + y, and the first server won (7 + y) + y = 7 + 2y points in total. This is an odd number, and only Smith won an odd number of points. Thus Smith served first.

19. White's key move of 1 Ka5!! seems self-destructive and a sure provocation for Black to play 1 … e1(Q)+. White's reply, 2 Kb6!, seems even more provocative as it offers Black no fewer than seven different moves with which to check White's king. Each one, however, can be defended by moving the knight at c6 for a discovered checkmate. If Black moves 1 … Rg7 then 2 Ne7+ Ka7 3 Nc8 mate. If 1 … Rg5 then 2 Kb6 (threatening 3 Ne7 mate) Rxd5 3 Nc7 mate. If 1 … Kb7 then 2 Ne7+ Ka7 3 Nc8 mate.

20. Forever and ever.

21. The envelope with the formula is Envelope 3.

22.

23. The series is generated by counting the number of characters in the corresponding Roman numeral, as shown for the first ten numbers below:

I	II	III	IV	V	VI	VII	VIII	IX	X
1	2	3	2	1	2	3	4	2	1

The first term to equal 10 is the 288th in the series: CCLXXXVIII. Thus the answer to the question is Brutus.

24. To show the perimeter is divided into two equal lengths, whatever the angle of the arrow, let the diameter of each of the smaller semicircles (and thus the radius of the large semicircle) be d and let the arrow lie at an angle of a radians to the horizontal.

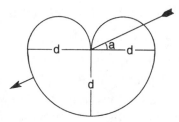

The perimeter length lying above the horizontal line is $\frac{\pi d}{2} + \frac{\pi d}{2} = \pi d$, which is the perimeter length lying below the horizontal line. Therefore, to prove the heart's perimeter is divided into two equal lengths, we need to show that the part of the perimeter above the horizontal line and below the arrow is equal in length to the part of the perimeter that is below the horizontal line and above the arrow.

Begin by letting C be the center of the smaller semicircle on the right as shown below:

Since triangle ABC is isosceles, angle BCD is 2a radians. Thus the length of arc BD is $\frac{2a}{2\pi}$ multiplied by the perimeter of the small circle $= \frac{2a}{2\pi} \times \pi d = ad$. This is also the length of the arc of the big semicircle that is below the horizontal line and above the arrow and so the result is proven.

25. Bend over backwards.

26. The new chart is shown below:

Last week		This week	Last week		This week
Atomic	1	Atomic	Valentine	21	Another Day
Blockbuster	2	Dizzy	What	22	Kayleigh
Classic	3	Footloose	Xanadu	23	Xanadu
Dizzy	4	Blockbuster	YMCA	24	Angie Baby
Emma	5	Jesamine	Zabadak!	25	True
Footloose	6	Classic	Autumn Almanac	26	Mickey
Gaye	7	Night	Angie Baby	27	YMCA
Hello	8	Perfect	Another Day	28	Valentine
Intuition	9	Lamplight	Angel Eyes	29	Angel Eyes
Jesamine	10	Emma	Angel Fingers	30	Ain't Nobody
Kayleigh	11	What	Amateur Hour	31	Amateur Hour
Lamplight	12	Obsession	Angela Jones	32	New entry
Mickey	13	Autumn Almanac	Ain't Nobody	33	Angel Fingers
Night	14	Gaye	American Pie	34	Question
Obsession	15	Reward	Ant Rap	35	Always Yours
Perfect	16	Hello	Alphabet Street	36	Adoration Waltz
Question	17	American Pie	Alternate Title	37	Alternate Title
Reward	18	Intuition	As Usual	38	Sandy
Sandy	19	As Usual	Adoration Waltz	39	Alphabet Street
True	20	Zabadak!	Always Yours	40	Angela Jones

27. Mixed bag.

28. ANGST, ABYSS, BAWDY, COMFY, DENIM, EXPEL, FAKIR, MAJOR, PIQUE, SERVE, TITLE, TOPAZ, WINCH.

29. The letter "m".

30. Either 1, 2, 6, 7, 9, 14, 15, 18, 20 or 1, 3, 6, 7, 12, 14, 15, 19, 20.

31. The minimum number of moves made by White's men to reach the position shown in the question is: queen's pawn 5 (d4, c5, b6, a7, a8), new queen 2 (a7, e3), queen's knight 2 (c3, a4), king's knight 2 (f3, h2), king's rook 2 (h3, g3), king's rook's pawn 2 (h3, g4), king's bishop's pawn 1 (f3) and king 1 (f2).

These total seventeen and therefore account for all of White's moves. Noting that Black's missing pieces were captured on c5, b6, a7, and g4, the position after White's ninth move would have been as follows:

The game from White's ninth move was:

9 …	Ra7
10 bxa 7	h4
11 a8(Q)	h3
12 Qa7	h2
13 Qe3	h1(B)
14 Nh2	a5
15 f3	a4
16 Kf2	a3
17 N	a4

32. The traveler on the fast train sees all the trains going the other way around that left up to three hours ago or that will leave in the next two hours. The traveler on the slow train sees all the trains going the other way around that left up to two hours ago or that will leave in the next three hours. In five hours, including the beginning and end, 21 trains depart in each direction. Including the train they are traveling on, each traveler therefore sees 22 trains on his journey.

33.

C	D	X	C	I	V	D
L	V	M	M	I	I	L
X	C	I	X	D	X	V
I	C	C	X	C	I	I
C	M	L	X	X	I	X
X	I	I	I	V	C	I
I	X	X	X	I	I	I

34. White marbles can only be removed from the box in pairs. There is an odd number of white marbles to start with, so the last marble in the box will be white.

35. At the point of no return.

36. There are 120 socks in the drawer: 85 red ones and 35 blue ones.

37. 72 hens, 21 sheep, 7 cows.

38. The value of 1,997 nickels is $99.85, 25 cents more than 1,992 nickels (worth $99.60).

39. Pin-up.

40. F for February. The letters are the initials of the first eight months of the year.

41. A won against B, C, and D with scores of 3 – 0, 1 – 0, and 2 – 1 respectively. B won against C with a score of 1 – 0 and tied D with a score of 1 – 1. C won against D with a score of 2 – 0.

42. Supplements to use are: 8, 12, 14, 17, 18, 19, 20, 21, 22, 23, 25, 26, 27, 29, 30, 31, 33, 35, 37, 39, 41, 43, 45, 47, and 49. They total 711.

43. The solutions are 1,872,549,630 and 7,812,549,630, and are derived as follows: The 5 and 0 can be placed immediately. The sixth digit must be 4. The seventh digit is odd (since every second digit must be even), so it must be 9. The eighth digit must be 6. The ninth digit must be 3. The third digit is 1 or 7, so the fourth digit must be 2. The first three digits are therefore 187 or 781.

44. One step forward, two steps back.

45. Each line describes the line above. For example, since line five is 1 1 1 2 2 1, which can be expressed as three 1s (3 1), two 2s (2 2), and one 1 (1 1), line six is 3 1 2 2 1 1.

The tenth line in the pyramid is therefore: 1 3 2 1 1 3 1 1 1 2 3 1 1 3 1 1 2 2 1 1.

46. Reading between the lines.

47. The solution to LAGER x 4 = REGAL is 21978 x 4 = 87912.

48. This puzzle is designed so that most people who see it will think (falsely) that the clues are missing. They think this because they mistake the clues for clue numbers. The clues cannot be the clue numbers, however, since for one thing the puzzle would not then be solvable, and for another the order of the clues has been muddled up.

Clue 21-Across is 21 or, in letters, TWENTY-ONE. Once this clue has been solved the rest are easy. The answer is shown below:

49. Bermuda Triangle.

50.

```
                                    1   4   5
        2   0   6 / 2   9   8   7   0
                    2   0   6
                    ─────────
                        9   2   7
                        8   2   4
                        ─────────
                        1   0   3   0
                        1   0   3   0
                        ─────────────
```

51. 8128.

52. Not eleven, but ten times. The times are between 1:00 and 2:00, between 2:00 and 3:00, and so on, ending with once between 10:00 and 11:00. It does not happen between 11:00 and 12:00, since it happens at exactly 12:00 (noon and midnight). The question excludes noon and midnight, so that occurrence doesn't count.

53. Just between you and me.

54. The maximum number of blocks in the set is 55.

If only three of the five available colors are used, then opposite faces of a block must have the same color. Thus by symmetry there is only one way in which a block can be painted with any three given colors, and there are ten different ways in which three colors can be chosen.

If four colors are used, then two pairs of opposite faces must each have the same color. By symmetry it doesn't matter which way around the other two faces are painted. The colors for the two pairs of matching faces can be chosen in ten different ways, and the other two colors can then be chosen in three ways, giving an overall total of 30 combinations.

Finally, if five colors are used then just one pair of opposite faces will have the same color. The remaining four colors can be arranged in three different ways, so using five colors gives a total of $5 \times 3 = 15$ combinations.

The maximum number of blocks in the set is therefore $10 + 30 + 15 = 55$.

55. There are 26 former committee members (9 of whom are women), 27 committee members, and 39 members who have never been on the committee. This gives a total of 92 members.

56. The series consists of the numbers of letters in the words one, two, three, etc.

57. The integers are −3, −1, and 1.

58. Regrouping the series as 1, 2, 4, 8, 16, 32, 64, 128, and 256, the next two terms in this series are 512 and 1024. The answer to the question is 5121.

59. Cornerstone.

60. Old is 30 and Young is 18.

61.

62. Five across is three factorial, which is SIX. Two-thirds of SIX or, more precisely, the last two-thirds of the word SIX, is IX, which is the Roman numeral nine.

63. Anyone for tennis?

64. Noting that the 3-5 domino can be placed uniquely, the full array is soon easily figured out, as shown.

1	2	6	1	6	3	4	5
3	3	6	4	3	2	5	4
3	0	6	0	3	1	2	2
0	5	5	4	6	5	0	2
0	2	5	1	5	0	0	1
6	4	3	4	4	1	1	1
2	2	6	4	5	0	3	6

65. The players scored 5, 7, 11, 13, 17, 19, 29, 31, 37, 41, and 43 goals. Their average was 23 goals.

66. Split-second timing.

67. Despite being the worst shot of the three, Arthur has the best chance of surviving, with a probability of .5222. Allwyn has the next best chance of surviving at .3, and Aitkins has the least chance at .1778.

Arthur's tactic will be to aim to miss if the other two are alive. This is because the other two, if they get the choice, will fire at each other rather than Arthur. This will leave Arthur with the first shot at the survivor. The reason that Allwyn would choose to fire at Aitkins rather than Arthur is that he would rather have Arthur shooting at him with a 50% hit rate than Aitkins with an 80% success rate. The decision for Aitkins to fire at Allwyn rather than Arthur, if he gets the choice, is because for Aitkins to fire successfully at Arthur would be to sign his own death warrant.

68. One foot in the grave.

69. The two possible ways of dividing the square are shown below:

 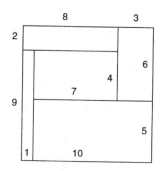

70. 93 and 87. When the digits in each number of the sequence are reversed, the sequence is the multiples of 13; that is, 13, 26, 39, 52, 65, 78, and 91.

71. $4! + 5! + 7! = 24 + 120 + 5040 = (5^2 - 1) + (11^2 - 1) + (71^2 - 1) = 72^2$.

72. By factorizing 2,450 and then compiling a list of the age groups with the desired product, it is found that only two have the same sum, namely 64. Thus Jim is 32, and the three passengers are either 50, 7, and 7 or 49, 10, and 5.

When he was told there was someone older than Bob on the bus, Jim was able to determine the passengers' ages. Obviously Bob cannot be older than 49, and if he were younger than this then both groups would still have been acceptable. Thus, knowing Bob was 49, Jim was able to determine the three passengers were aged 50, 7, and 7.

73. Mate in three can be forced only by 1 d4.

If 1 ... Kh5 then 2 Qd3 Kg4 (or Kh4) 3 Qh3 mate.

If 1 ... Kg4 then 2 e4+ Kh4 3 g3 mate.

74. This is H.E. Dudeney's solution:

1	Nc3	d5
2	Nxd5	Nc6
3	Nxe7	g5
4	Nxc8	Nf6
5	Nxa7	Ne4
6	Nxc6	Nc3
7	Nxd8	Rg8
8	Nxf7	Rg6
9	Nxg5	Re6
10	Nxh7	Nb1
11	Nxf8	Ra3
12	Nxe6	b5
13	Nxc7+	Kf7
14	Nxb5	Kg6
15	Nxa3	Kh5
16	Nxb1	Kh4

75. ♠2, ♥9, ♥5, ♦4, ♣8.

76. West Indies.

77. Sweet tooth.

78. On the double.

79.

O			X		
			X		
		O			
	X		X		
			O	O	

80. $6 / (1 - \frac{5}{7}) = 21$.

81. $96,420 \times 87,531 = 8,439,739,020$.

82. Income tax.

83. The diagram contains 47 triangles in total, as below:

1 triangle of full size, 6 triangles of $\frac{1}{2}$ size;

3 triangles of $\frac{1}{3}$ size, 10 triangles of $\frac{1}{4}$ size;

6 triangles of $\frac{1}{6}$ size, 12 triangles of $\frac{1}{8}$ size;

3 triangles of $\frac{1}{12}$ size, 6 triangles of $\frac{1}{24}$ size.

84. My father was born in 1927 ($2^{11} - 11^2$), and his grandfather in 1844 ($3^7 - 7^3$).

85. Receding hairline.

86.

$$
\begin{array}{r}
66.375 \\
16 \overline{)1062} \\
96 \\
\hline
102 \\
96 \\
\hline
60 \\
48 \\
\hline
120 \\
112 \\
\hline
80 \\
80 \\
\hline
\end{array}
$$

87. Four and three. The numbers are the numbers of letters in the words of the question.

88.

Position	Team	Captain	Color
1	United	Cooke	Red
2	Rovers	Allen	Blue
3	County	Dixon	White
4	Albion	Evans	Yellow
5	Thistle	Boyle	Green

89. Unfinished symphony.

90. Other than rotations and reflections there is only one solution. The best way to start is with the central number, which must be a factor of 45, the sum of all nine numbers.

5	1	4
6	3	8
2	7	9

91. Forgive and forget.

92. $50{,}123 - 49{,}876 = 247$.

93. If this position had occurred in a real game, then Black's last move must have been g^7-g^5. Therefore, White can force mate in two with **1** hxg6 e.p. Kh5 **2** Rxh7 mate.

94.

3	6	1
5	2	9
7	8	4

95. Digital Root $(9^{6130} + 2)^{4875}$

$= $ Digital Root $(2^{4875} + 9 \times$ (large number))

$= $ Digital Root $(8^{1625} + 9)$

$= $ Digital Root $((9 - 1)^{1625} + 9)$

$= $ Digital Root $((9 \times$ (large number) $- 1) + 9)$

$= $ Digital Root $(9 - 1 + 9) = 8$

96. To prove this, color the large triangle of 36 units in area as shown, giving 21 light and 15 dark unit triangles.

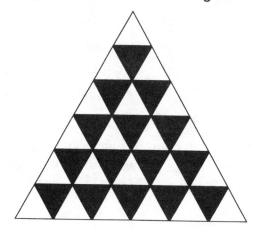

If the twelve available shapes are colored in a similar manner, ten are found to have an equal number of light and dark unit triangles. In the remaining two cases, there are four light and two dark (or vice versa). However, to tile the shape above requires at least three pieces where the difference between the numbers of light and dark triangles is two. Since there are only two such pieces, no solution is possible.

97. The two hands clearly cannot occur in the same deal, so we compare the number of hands that beat these two. They are both beaten by the same number of four-of-a-kinds, but the first hand is beaten by 32 straight flushes, the second by 31. Hence the full house with the three kings is the stronger hand.

98. Regrouping the sequence as 20, 21, 22, 23, 24, 25, 26, 27, 28, it is obvious the next three terms in this more normal format are 29, 30, and 31. Using the question's format, the required answer is 293 and 031.

99. Space Invaders.

100. 18, since $18^3 = 5,832$ and $18^4 = 104,976$.

101. Maverick, subtle (or bustle), pique, golfer, jinx, wrap, brazen, and holiday.

102. The verse asks whether $10^{1/10} > 2^{1/3}$ or, if we raise each side to the power of 30, whether $10^3 > 2^{10}$? The answer is "no."

103.

	M	C	C	C	L	X	I	X
M	M	M	D	C		X		L
C	M			L	X	X	X	I
C	X	L	I	V		V		X
X	X	X	V	I		I	X	C
X	V	I			M		L	X
V		V		C	D		I	X
		M	M	C	M	X	V	I

104. Back and forth.

105. Let the radii of the larger and smaller circles be R and r, respectively. The desired area is then $\pi R^2 - \pi r^2 = \pi(R^2 - r^2)$.

Using the Pythagorean theorem, it can be seen that $R^2 - r^2 = \left(\frac{24}{2}\right)^2 = 144$, so the desired area is $144\pi = 452.4$ sq. cm.

106. By crossing out "SIX LETTERS," we are left with the word "BANANA."

107. Weeping willow.

108. $325 = 1^2 + 18^2 = 6^2 + 17^2 = 10^2 + 15^2$.

109. The base n of the measurements can be found using the Pythagorean theorem, which gives the following decimal equation: $7^2 + (2n)^2 = (n + 3)^2 + (n + 8)^2$, from which n = 12. Thus the base being used in the question is 12, and using this base, the hypotenuse measures 21. In base ten the sides are 7, 24, and 25, and 15, 20, and 25.

110. Let the radius of the largest ball that will fit in the gap be r, and let the distance from the corner to the center of the smaller ball be y.

The distance from the corner to the center of the big ball is $20 + r + y = \sqrt{(20^2 + 20^2)}$, so $r + y = \sqrt{800} - 20 = 8.28$ cm. Since $y = \sqrt{(r^2 + r^2)}$, $2r^2 = (8.28 - r)^2$, from which $r^2 + 16.57r - 68.63 = 0$ and $r = 3.43$ cm. This means that the largest ball that can fit in the gap has diameter $2 \times 3.43 = 6.86$ cm, so the answer to the original question is no.

111. Count Dracula.

112. Long underwear.

113. 1 bxa8(N) Kxg2 2 Nb6 any 3 a8(B or Q) mate. Note that White's second move prevents 2 … Bxa7.

114. Queueing.

115. At least two blocks are featured. The first five views are all consistent with each other, but the sixth is not. The "Z" on the upper face would have to be a "U" (with its base at the edge adjoining the face with the "E") for this block to match the others.

116. See-through blouse.

117. $123 - 45 - 67 + 89 = 100$.

118. 3,782,915,460.

119. Let the width of the star be 2a, and construct a line from the center of the star (and circle) to where one of the two outer threads meets the circle.

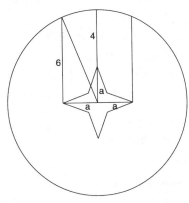

Clearly, the radius of the circle is 4 + a. The diagonal line is a radius, but it is also the hypotenuse of a right-angled triangle with sides of length 6 and a. Thus by the Pythagorean theorem we have $6^2 + a^2 = (4 + a)^2$, so a equals 2.5 cm and the width of the star is 5 cm.

120. Safety in numbers.

121. I would not want a tiger to chase me or a zebra to chase me. Given the choice, I'd rather a tiger chased a zebra, not me.

122. Rewriting each ANNE in base ten, we have:
$$A(8^3 - 5^3 - 7^3) + N(8^2 + 8 - 5^2 - 5 - 7^2 - 7) + E(1 - 1 - 1) = 0$$
That is, $44A - 14N - E = 0$. Noting that A, N, and E are all digits of a number written in base five, so A, N, and E are all less than five, A = 1, N = 3, and E = 2 is the unique solution. Thus the three letters do represent three different digits.

123.

124. Crossroads.

125. Black's last move was a7-a5. It could not have been a6-a5 since a pawn at a6 would have had to capture White's pawn. Neither could it have been b6xa5 since this would imply, given the position of Black's other pawns, that Black had made nine captures (which is impossible since White still has eight pieces on the board). Thus White plays **1** bxa6 e.p.

White wins by being stalemated as follows: **1** … bxa6 **2** b5 axb5 **3** f5 any, and White is stalemated.

126. In the adjacent diagram, the two smaller triangles are similar, which means the ratio of their sides is constant, and more particularly, that $\frac{y}{1} = \frac{1}{x}$.

By the Pythagorean theorem:
$(x + 1)^2 + (y + 1)^2 = (x + 1)^2 + (\frac{1}{x} + 1)^2 = 25$, so
$x^4 + 2x^3 + 2x^2 + 2x + 1 = 25x^2$, from which
$(x^2 + x + 1)^2 = 26x^2$, so $x^2 + (1 - \sqrt{26})x + 1 = 0$ and
$x = 0.2605$ meters.

The base of the ladder is 1.2605 meters from the wall.

127.

8	1	1	2	3	4	2
4	2	6	8	0	8	4
4	2	2	4	1	6	2
5	6	8	0	2	4	4
2	1	4	1	5	0	6
2	4	5	2	7	4	8
4	2	2	2	6	2	4

128. Five thousand.

129. Out of court.

130.

131. The terms in the series are one hundred in base ten, one hundred in base nine, one hundred in base eight, . . . , one hundred in base five. The next term in the series is one hundred in base four, which is 1210.

132. The letters are the first letters of the words in the question. Thus the next two letters are A and W.

133. Construct another regular five-pointed star as shown in the diagram. Since both are regular stars, $\frac{AB}{BC} = \frac{AD}{DB}$.

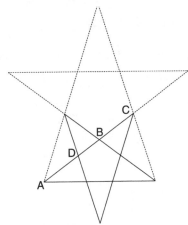

Let AB be of unit length and AD = BC = x (so DB = 1 − x). Then: $\frac{AB}{BC} = \frac{AD}{DB}$ so $\frac{1}{x} = \frac{x}{(1-x)}$.

So $x^2 + x - 1 = 0$, $x = -\frac{1}{2} + \frac{1}{2}\sqrt{5} = 0.618034$, and the ratio of AB to BC is the reciprocal of 0.618034, which is 1.618034.

134. The values of A, B, and C are 1111, 2222, and 5555, respectively, and the question is whether $B^C + C^B$ is divisible by 7.

$$B^C + C^B = (B^C + C^B) + (4^C - 4^B) - (4^C - 4^B)$$
$$= (B^C + 4^C) + (C^B - 4^B) - 4^B(64^A - 1^A)$$

Since C is odd, $(B^C + 4^C)$ is divisible by (B + 4), which is divisible by 7. $(C^B - 4^B)$ is divisible by (C − 4), which is divisible by 7. Lastly, $4^B(64^A - 1^A)$ is divisible by (64 − 1), which is divisible by 7. Thus $B^C + C^B$ is divisible by 7.

135.

		7	7	5
			3	3
	2	3	2	5
2	3	2	5	
2	5	5	7	5

136. Too few to mention.

137. 916.

138. The three names are Arnold, Roland, and Ronald.

139. 1 Qe6+ Kh8 2 Nf7+ Kg8 3 Nh6+ Kh8 4 Qg8+ Rxg8 5 Nf7 mate.

140. Construct the line CG as shown below:

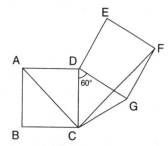

Since DC = DG and angle CDG is 60°, triangle CDG is equilateral, so DC = DG = CG.

Thus, triangle CGF is isosceles, since CG = GF. Angle CGF is angle CGD + angle DGF, which is 60° + 90°, or 150°. So angles GCF and GFC are both 15°.

Since angle DCG is 60° and angle GCF is 15°, angle FCD is 45°. Angle ACD is also 45°, so angle ACF is the sum of FCD and ACD, or 45° + 45°, which is 90°.

141. The hands on the clock face show roughly when Heather left her room. The hour hand has moved (x − 35) minutes since 7 p.m., and the minute hand y minutes. Since the minute hand moves twelve times faster than the hour hand, y = 12(x − 35).

Now consider the position when the hands have changed places. The hour hand will have moved (y – 50) minutes since 10 p.m., and the minute hand x minutes. Hence x = 12(y – 50). Solving these equations, x = $39\frac{63}{143}$ and y = $53\frac{41}{143}$. Thus the time elapsed since Heather left her room was 2 hours 46 minutes $9\frac{3}{13}$ seconds.

142. Laid back.

143. 6174.

144. Let the longer candle burn at L $^{cm}/_{hr}$ and the shorter candle at S $^{cm}/_{hr}$. Then the longer candle was 8L cm, the shorter candle 8.75S cm, and 8L = 8.75S + 2.
At 8 p.m. the candles were the same length, so 4L = 5S. Solving with the above, S = $\frac{8}{5}$ and L = 2, so the longer candle was 16 cm and the shorter candle was 14 cm.

145. *Little House on the Prairie.*

146. The pairs are:

$\frac{355}{113}$ = 3.1415929…   (π = 3.1415926…)

$\frac{577}{408}$ = 1.414215…   ($\sqrt{2}$ = 1.414213…)

$\frac{878}{323}$ = 2.71826…   (e = 2.71828…)

$\frac{987}{610}$ = 1.618032…   (ϕ = 1.618033…)

where π is the area of a circle of unit radius, e is the base for natural logarithms, and ϕ is the golden ratio. Interesting properties of ϕ include its relationship with its square (which equals ϕ + 1) and its reciprocal (which equals ϕ – 1). ϕ = (1 + $\sqrt{5}$) / 2.

147. The four ages are 12, 16, 42, and 44.

148. Split level.

149. The number at the center of any 3 x 3 magic square is always one-third of the magic square's constant. Thus the center square must be 37. The rest then follows. (Reflected and rotated answers are also possible.)

43	1	67
61	37	13
7	73	31

150. "We" are the number of letters in each word. Thus "twelve" is six, "nine" is four, etc.

151. ABCDE is 93084.

152. The key move is 1 Bh3, to which Black must reply with a queen move. If Black plays **1 … Qa8** or **1 … Qe8**, then **2 Qd4+ Qe4 3 Qf6+ Qf5 4 Qg5+ Qxg5** mate.

If Black keeps his queen on the same rank, say **1 … Qd4,** then **2 g3+ Kf3+ 3 Bg4+ Qxg4** mate.

If Black plays any other queen move, then White plays either **2 Qb4+** or **2 Qc4+** or **2 Qd4+** forcing Black to reply with either **2 … Qxb4** or **2 … Qxc4** or **2 … Qxd4** and then White forces Black to win as above. For example, **1 Bh3 Qa6 2 Qc4+Qxc4 3 g3+ Kf3+ 4 Bg4+ Qxg4** mate.

153. Bob up and down.

154. Of all possible sets of four whole numbers whose product is 180, the only sets with sums that are not unique are those with sums of 18 and 22. Thus the professor must have been teaching for one of those two periods.

If it is 18 years, then the four lengths of study could be 1, 5, 6, and 6 years; 2, 2, 5, and 9 years; or 2, 3, 3, and 10 years. If it is 22 years, then the possible combinations are 1, 2, 9, and 10 years, or 2, 2, 3, and 15 years.

We are told that knowing whether any of the students were into double figures would enable the professor to determine the four periods, so a length of teaching of 22 years is ruled out. Of the three sets whose sum is 18 years, two contain no double-digit numbers, which leaves the third set as the only possibility.

Thus the four students had been studying for 2, 3, 3, and 10 years.

155. There is no choice regarding the queen and king; each has only one square on which to be placed. The rooks, knights, and bishops can each be positioned in two ways, giving a total of $2^3 = 8$ different combinations. The eight pawns can be positioned in 8! = 40,320 ways. Thus for the pieces of one color there are a total of 8 x 40,320 = 322,560 possibilities.

156. Lucky break.

157. The positions were first, fifth, and ninth for the navy; second, sixth, and seventh for the air force; and third, fourth, and eighth for the army.

158. Three wise men.

159. 1 d4 d5 2 Qd3 Qd6 3 Qh3 Qh6 4 Qxc8 mate.

160. Monday is an anagram of dynamo.

161. The middle of nowhere.

162. Robin Hood.

MIGHTY MIND BOGGLERS

MIND BOGGLER

Here's a quick brainteaser: What is special about the grid below—
and what is missing from it?

Answer, page 372

U	R	O	W
O	N	G	T
F	I	E	H
X	V	S	R

TYING THE KNOT

According to an ancient custom, if a woman throws five ropes out of a high window, and three or more of them land such that they will form knots when both ends are pulled, she will be married within the next year. The ropes here show one woman's tosses. Should she expect a wedding this year?

Answer, page 377

1.

2.

3.

4.

5.

TECHNIQUE-COLOR

Jo is making a stained-glass window, and she wants each adjacent piece of glass to be a different color. She wants to use just four colors: yellow, orange, purple, and red.

   If the center circle is yellow, and two other pieces are colored as shown, what color does piece A need to be?

Answer, page 376

ANIMAL STRENGTH

If the first two tug of war contests shown here are ties, which group will win the third contest, or will it also be a draw?

Answer, page 367

1.

2.

3.

THEORY OF RELATIVITY

At the Embee family reunion, your sister is talking to your grandmother Mary, your cousin Bo, and your uncle Bill. Who are you?

Answer, page 376

PAPER CLIP FLIP

Most of the wire sculptures below were made from standard paper clips, by twisting them at existing bends.

Which of the shapes could not have been made by bending the original paper clip?

Answer, page 373

12-STEP PROGRAM

Work through the code of this computer program, line by line. Your output will answer this riddle: WHAT DID COWBOY DAVE HAVE TO DO BEFORE GOING TO THE COMPUTER USERS' DANCE?

01 Set Number = 1
02 Set Letter at (Number) = "P"
03 Number = Number + 3
04 Set Letter at (Number) = "O"
05 Number = Number + 1
06 If Number £5 go to line 04
07 Set Letter at (Number) = "B"
08 Number = Number ÷ 3
09 Set Letter at (Number) = "U"
10 Number = Number + 1
11 Set Letter at (Number) = "T"
12 Reverse the output

Output:

_____
1   2   3   4   5   6

Answer, page 377

THIRTEEN CANDLES

Claude doesn't want anyone to know how old he is unless they do some work. So he designed a birthday cake that uses 13 candles and represents his age.

    If you count all of the triangles of all sizes formed by the lines connecting the candles, you will discover Claude's age. Can you figure it out before the candles are blown out?

Answer, page 376

HAIRY TALES

1. Rapunzel's hair grew 100 feet longer while waiting to be saved by the prince. Hair grows one inch every two months.
So, how long had the fair maiden been trapped in the tower when she was rescued?

2. In Washington Irving's story, Rip Van Winkle's beard grew two feet in the 20 years that he slept. Is the story accurate?

Answer, page 370

KEEP THE FAITH

The eruptions of the Old Faithful geyser are indeed very predictable. Below are the last five eruptions:

1. at 12:00 p.m. for five minutes
2. at 12:50 p.m. for six minutes
3. at 1:44 p.m. for seven minutes
4. at 2:42 p.m. for eight minutes
5. at 3:44 p.m. for nine minutes

Can you calculate when the next eruption will be?

Answer, page 371

259

BLOCK PARTY

The alphabet blocks below are of two different types, turned around in various positions. No letter appears on both types of block. The letters on the underside of the blocks spell out the answer to this riddle:

HOW DID BARBIE GET THROUGH THE PILE OF ALPHABET BLOCKS?

Can you do some mental tumbling and figure out the solution?

Answer, page 367

She took the . . .

SELF TEST

The answers to the questions below are one-digit numbers from one to nine, and no number is repeated. Can you figure out the unique set of answers?

1. Answer to statement 5 minus answer to statement 4.
2. Answer to statement 8 times answer to statement 9.
3. Answer to statement 4 plus answer to statement 8.
4. Number of times that the number 9 is an answer.
5. Total number of statements.
6. Answer to statement 1 minus answer to statement 4.
7. Number of odd answers.
8. Answer to statement 2 divided by answer to statement 9.
9. Answer to statement 6 minus answer to statement 7.

Answer, page 374

LOSING TRACK

On this animal track quiz, one student copied his or her answers from the other three students. By looking at their answers below, you should be able to tell who cheated.

Ironically, the cheater got none of the answers correct. If the other students had two correct answers each, what are the correct answers?

The Question:
Match these five tracks to the animals that made them.

The Answers:
ART: 1. deer 2. caribou 3. mt. goat 4. moose 5. bison
BOB: 1. caribou 2. moose 3. deer 4. bison 5. mt. goat
CAT: 1. bison 2. mt. goat 3. deer 4. caribou 5. moose
DEB: 1. deer 2. moose 3. mt. goat 4. caribou 5. bison

Answer, page 371

1   2   3   4   5

BLIND ALLEYS

On his birthday, Joe's friends blindfolded him and took him for a drive. If they took two right turns, a left turn, and another left, and ended up at Wally World, where did they start?

Answer, page 367

GRAPHIC LANGUAGE

Find the letters that correspond to the coordinates given below. Write them in order on the dashes to answer this riddle: WHY WAS SIX AFRAID OF SEVEN?

1. C5
2. G3
3. A3
4. D5
5. F2
6. A1
7. D2
8. F4
9. B4
10. E6
11. B6
12. C3
13. A5
14. E1

	A	B	C	D	E	F	G
6	D	N	R	Y	T	M	F
5	N	L	S	E	O	K	Z
4	P	H	J	C	B	G	A
3	V	O	I	R	U	W	E
2	U	M	X	I	T	N	P
1	E	A	G	Q	E	S	L

Answer:
BECAUSE _ _ _ _ _ _ _ _ _ _ _ _ _ _ _ _ _ _ .

Answer, page 370

264

PRODUCE PRODUCTS

The numbers one through nine are represented by nine different vegetables in the equations below. Each veggie represents the same number throughout. If the broccoli equals 3, what is the identity of the carrot?

Answer, page 373

onion − broccoli = pea pod

mushroom + bell pepper = chili pepper

bell pepper × lettuce = tomato

pea pod ÷ broccoli = lettuce

carrot = ?

WHAT'S THE PLAN?

Which three-dimensional object at the bottom does the simple orthographic projection above it represent?

Answer, page 377

TOP

FRONT

FRACTION WORDS

Add the parts of words below as indicated to come up with two answer words. In each case, use the first letters of the word in your addition. For example, one-third of CAT would be C.

　　　Both solutions answer this riddle: What has keys, but can't open a door?

Answer, page 369

A.

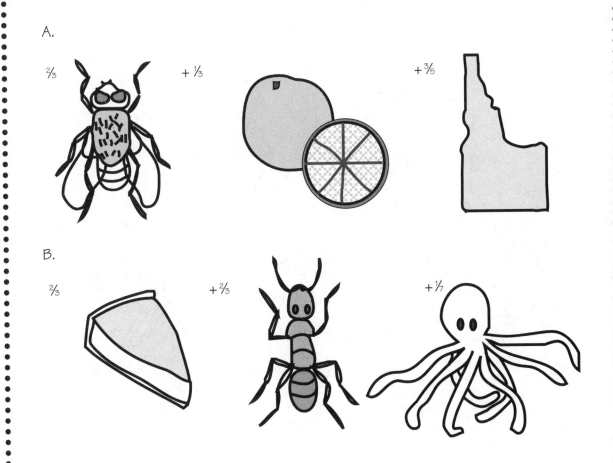

⅔　　　　+ ⅓　　　　　　　　+ ⅗

B.

⅔　　　　+ ⅔　　　　　　　　+ ⅐

267

THREE HEXES

Most of the shapes here can be made by combining three equal-sized hexagons. Which ones cannot?

Answer, page 376

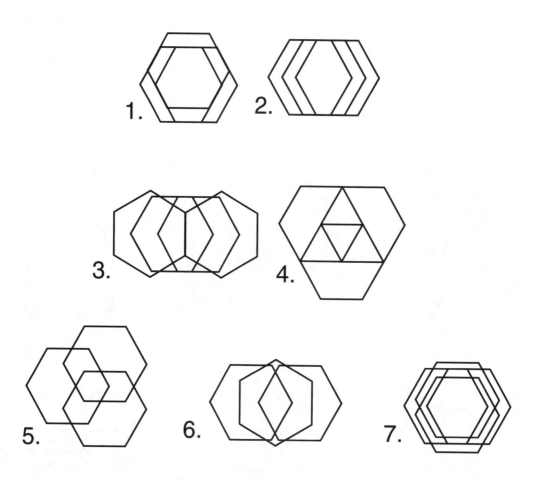

1.   2.

3.   4.

5.   6.   7.

WINTER EYES

To make simple snowflakes, fold a square of paper into quarters, cut shapes, and unfold. Which folded snowflakes (1–7) will unfold to create snowflakes A, B, and C?

Answer, page 377

1

2

3

4

5

6

7

A

B

C

TEN GOLD COINS

Ten gold coins are hidden under ten of the unlabeled hexagonal tiles in this floor. The numbers on the labeled tiles indicate how many coins are under tiles adjacent to that tile.

Can you locate the ten gold coins without looking under any of the wrong tiles?

Answer, page 376

MIRROR IMAGES

Using only a square mirror and the jigsaw shape below, most of the figures below can be formed. Which figures are impossible? (Remember, parts of the new shapes are seen in the mirror.)

Answer, page 372

271

FISHING FOR WORDS

Remove words from the nonsense paragraph below as instructed. When you are done, the words that remain will spell out a Spanish proverb.

THOUGH FEROCIOUS THE GREEN TURTLE SPIT LOWER FISH STRESSED BARREL DIES GULP BECAUSE HE EAR CANNOT PLUG OPENS RIGHT INK HIS TEN WHISTLING TIPS SHARKS NET MOUTH LAKE DESSERTS.

1. Remove all of the words that are between two words that begin with a T.

2. Take away all of the pairs of words that spell each other backward.

3. Cross out all of the words that become another word when an F is added before the first letter.

4. Remove all of the six-letter words.

Answer, page 369

272

GOT CLASS?

It's time to put together your class schedule for next semester's classes. You need to take two science classes, one math or computer class, one English class, and one history. Given the list of classes that sound interesting to you, which combination of class times will work? (R is Thursday.)

American history	TRF 9:05-10:00
Biology	TR 8:00-10:00
Calculus	MW 11:15-1:15
English lit	TR 9:05-10:00
European history	MWF 10:10-11:05
Genetics	MWF 12:20-1:15
PC basics	TR 12:20-1:15
Physics	MWF 10:10-11:05
Shakespeare	TR 11:15-1:15
Statistics	MWF 8:00-9:10

Answer, page 370

NEXT IN LINE

The four pictures below form a logical sequence in order from left to right. Can you figure out what links one picture to the next and then deduce which of the three objects (a, b, or c) below comes next in the line?

Answer, page 372

1.   2.   3.   4.

a.

b.

c.

MATCH BOXES

Which pieces of cardboard below will form boxes if they are folded along the lines?

Answer, page 372

A GOOD EGG

Ostriches lay the largest eggs in the world. To find out how many omelets can be made from one ostrich egg, solve the word puzzle below. (Each omelet uses the equivalent of two hen's eggs.)

Spell the six-letter answer as described:
1. A letter in EGRET but not GREBE
2. A letter in CROW but not CONDOR
3. A letter in WARBLER but not BARN OWL
4. A letter in KESTREL, EAGLE, and FALCON
5. A letter in RAVEN but not CRANE
6. A letter in PIGEON, WREN, and OSPREY

_ _ _ _ _ _

Answer, page 370

SEA OR SOIL?

The good news is that your rich uncle Charlie has bequeathed to you a treasure map. The bad news is that it has been ripped on all four sides, so that you have only the key piece.

You are told that there is a treasure buried at point X and that point A is on land. If the area is composed of one lake and the land around it, and there are no islands in the lake, is the treasure under sea or under land?

Answer, page 374

BERRY IMPRESSIVE

A new, genetically engineered strawberry clones itself every month, except for the first month, when it is dormant. Each new strawberry is identical to the first one in that it, too, clones itself every month after being dormant for a month. If one of these new strawberries is planted at the beginning of March and harvested at the beginning of November, how many berries will result?

Answer, page 367

FISHING LINES

Today, eight people are trying to hook some trout on this part of the Lazy River.

Fishermen like to fish their own holes. To separate everyone, draw two straight lines across the map so that each fisher is on his or her own piece of river. Can you find a way for Mac to fish on his own piece of river? What about Bill?

Answer, page 369

AGES OF REASON

Aunt Pearl doesn't like to tell anyone her age, but she will say this:

"In Roman numerals, my age is made up of one I, one V, one L, and one X. My age is the second largest number that can be made from those symbols. My daughter's age is the second smallest number that can be made from those symbols."

How old is Pearl and how old is your cousin?

Answer, page 367

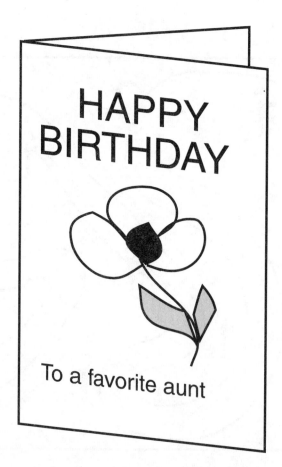

HAPPY
BIRTHDAY

To a favorite aunt

BLACK AND WHITE

In this game, you can see your friends' cards, but not your own. If there are four black cards and four white cards to choose from, can you deduce which cards you have by what the other players know?

Answer, page 367

1. Friend A   Friend B   You

Neither Friend A, Friend B, nor you know what you have. Then, friend A says she knows. What cards do you have?

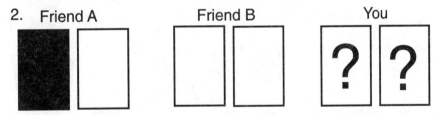

2. Friend A   Friend B   You

Neither Friend A, Friend B, or you know what you have. Then, Friend A still doesn't know. What cards do you have?

SLICE OF LIFE

Your meatball pizza just came out of the oven and now you need to feed six hungry kids. These kids are picky, so they each want the same number of meatballs. They also each want the same size piece of pizza. How can you cut the pie to satisfy all six kids?

Answer, page 375

FOR YOUR THOUGHTS

1. Which circle below is the size of a penny?

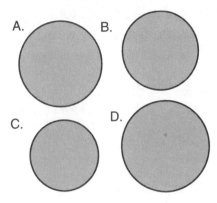

A. B.

C. D.

2. How many pennies, stacked on their sides, equal the diameter of one penny?

    A. eight B. ten C. twelve D. fourteen

Answers, page 369

GAME PLAN

In these super tic-tac-toe games, the letters are entered from the top of the board, so that only the lowest empty box in each column can be played. If it's O's turn in game A and X's turn in game B, who should win each game? (Three X's or O's in a row wins.)

Answer, page 369

A.

B.

284

SHIFTING GEARS

In each case, which way will gear C turn?

Answer, page 374

TO THE LETTER

All of the eight shapes below are parts of the 26 letters shown above them, although they may have been enlarged and rotated. Figure out which letter each shape was taken from. The answers, in order, will spell a word.

Answer, page 376

abcdefghijklm
nopqrstuvwxyz

IRISH EYES

Can you find the four-leaf clover in this field? Good luck!

Answer, page 371

KEY RINGS

In each group below, if any one of the rings were picked up, would all of the other rings be lifted with it?

Answer, page 371

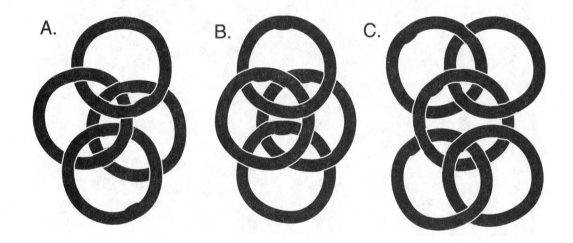

A.   B.   C.

JOLLOS AND PLOTZ

These are jollos:

These are plotz:

Which are jollos and which are plotz?

A.   B.   C.   D.   E.

Answer, page 371

289

IT'S ABOUT TIME

Match each definition to a clock shown below.

1. Snack time
2. Work time
3. Flight time
4. Tax time
5. Height time
6. Class time

Answer, page 371

A.   B.   C.

D.   E.   F.

FAMILIAR FACES

Which of these familiar faces are facing the correct way, and which are mirror images?

Answer, page 369

DETECTIVE STORY

"Detective Slooth? This is Sergeant Chiller from Thunder Bay. We have been tracking a jewelry thief and he's headed south toward you. He is driving a red Honda Civic above the speed limit and he's dressed for the weather, which is 30 degrees. I hope you can help us intercept him before he pawns off the goods."

Detective Slooth sees a red Honda Civic coming into Duluth, but the driver is wearing shorts and a tank top. What should he do?

Answer, page 368

COFFEE BREAK

Sally decided she wanted to give up coffee. She thought she would drink tea instead, until she read that one pound of black tea contains twice as much caffeine as one pound of coffee.

However, Sally should also know that one pound of tea yields about 160 cups, whereas one pound of coffee makes about 40 cups. One 12-ounce can of cola has about one-quarter of the caffeine of a cup of coffee.

How much caffeine is in a cup of tea, relative to a cup of coffee and to a can of cola?

Answer, page 368

TOUGH COOKIES

Joey's mom brought out a plate of cookies for him and four friends. Unfortunately, there was one cookie too many to divide them evenly. Then, Ben came in and they figured that each of them could get the same number of cookies. The kids were just about to eat when Sarah came through the door. Sadly, the cookies could not be divided evenly any more. But Joey pointed out that if they gave one to his mom, the rest would divide evenly. How many cookies were on the plate? (Hint: There were fewer than 100.)

Answer, page 376

PAPER PINBALL

Begin at IN (10 points) and move along the lines to OUT (5 points), calculating as you go to get a high score. You may hit a bumper twice, but you may not trace over any part of your path. Our high score is 295. Can you beat it?

Answer, page 373

CATEGORICALLY SPEAKING

The 25 words below are the answers to a game of Categories. That is, each of them fits one of five categories and begins with one of five letters. Can you reconstruct the categories and arrange the words so that each category contains a word beginning with each letter?

Answer, page 367

MAGENTA CORAL MANGO

AMETHYST SHELL CHESTNUT

SNOWBALL PURPLE MUSSEL

CANDY CAMELLIA SPRUCE

ANEMONE MAGNOLIA PAIL

PALM SAND SCARLET CHAIR

MYRTLE AMARYLLIS APPLE

PEARL PRIMROSE AMBER

GET THE SCOOP

Ken and Terry's, the local ice cream shop, will be giving away free cones some time this year. Because they want to limit the lines a bit, they have given out three clues as to the date of their giveaway. Can you figure out when it will be?

- The giveaway will be in the first week of a month without an A in it.
- It will be on a day of the week that has a U in it.
- The month has no E but the day of the week contains an E.

Answer, page 369

FIT FOR A PRINCESS

Young Princess Figleaf of Lalaland has four pieces of jewelry that are family heirlooms: a necklace, a ring, a bracelet, and a brooch. Being a fashion-conscious noble, she doesn't like to wear the same thing twice.

How many different combinations of crown jewels can Princess Figleaf wear? She may wear any number of jewels at a time.

Answer, page 369

RUFF AND READY

At the recent running of the Doggie Jog, every person ran with at least one dog. The organizers want to know how many dogs and people participated. Unfortunately, the photographer tripped as he took the group picture and got a shot of the racers' feet, but nothing else. A reporter in a helicopter scanned the canines and humans from above, but his scanner picked up only the total number of eyes. If the photographer counted 196 feet and paws and the reporter tallied 126 eyes, how many people and how many dogs ran the race?

Answer, page 374

GLOBAL ECONOMY

While on a round-the-world trip, Wally priced the new Whales CD in eight countries. In which country should he buy the CD to get the best deal?

Answer, page 370

COST OF CD
Here's what the CD costs in each country:

90 francs
1,265 yen
420 rupees
70.2 kronor
18.2 Canadian dollars
17,000 lire
158 pesos
59.4 Egyptian pounds

EXCHANGE RATES
One American dollar buys:

1.3 Canadian dollars
6.0 French francs
1,700 Italian lire
7.8 Swedish kronor
7.9 Mexican pesos
3.3 Egyptian pounds
35 Indian rupees
115 Japanese yen

The Whales

Spout

NOVEL IDEA

Follow the directions here very carefully, and you will find a humorous ending to this sentence starter:
AUTHORS ARE ALL . . .

1.   Take out all the spaces, and remove the O.
2.   Replace the two-letter postal code for a western state with a W.
3.   Add two Ds at the very end.
4.   Add "THE" between the E and the A.
5.   Add an N between any repeated letters.
6.   Add an I before the second A and a T after the A.
7.   Add the word ME before the last two letters.
8.   Delete every odd letter (the first, third, etc.).
9.   Add a space and read the answer.

Answer, page 372

ALLIGATOR ALLY

Use logic to figure out which is the alligator and which is the crocodile. One of them is telling the truth and one is lying.

Answer, page 367

The alligator's bottom tooth shows when it closes its mouth.

I am telling the truth.

Alligators and crocodiles can go for two years without eating.

The alligator is lying.

GIVE ME FIVE

Believe it or not, five twos equal five. So do five threes. And five fours.
Insert symbols for addition, subtraction, multiplication, and division into the formulas below to make each equation true. You may also use parentheses. The first equation is filled in for you.

$$(2 \times 2 \times 2 + 2) \div 2 = 5$$
$$3 \quad 3 \quad 3 \quad 3 \quad 3 = 5$$
$$4 \quad 4 \quad 4 \quad 4 \quad 4 = 5$$
$$5 \quad 5 \quad 5 \quad 5 \quad 5 = 5$$
$$6 \quad 6 \quad 6 \quad 6 \quad 6 = 5$$
$$7 \quad 7 \quad 7 \quad 7 \quad 7 = 5$$
$$8 \quad 8 \quad 8 \quad 8 \quad 8 = 5$$
$$9 \quad 9 \quad 9 \quad 9 \quad 9 = 5$$

Answer, page 369

HULA HOOPLA

The simple arithmetic problems below are spelled out in Hawaiian. If all of the words represent one-digit numbers and are not 0 or 1, can you figure out the solution to the last equation?

HAWAIIAN EQUATIONS:
1. e'lua x e'lua + e'lima = e'iwa
2. e'walu ÷ e'ha x e'lua = e'ha
3. e'iwa ÷ e'kolu + e'kolu = e'ono
4. e'lua + e'ono − e'kolu = ??

Answer, page 370

RUNED PUNCH LINE

Can you decipher this joke and its punch line, which are written in a runic alphabet?

Answer, page 374

ᚹᚺᚨᛏ ᚺᛁᚺ ᚦᛖ ᛋᛁᚨᛗᛖᚾ ᚷᛖᛏ

ᚹᚺᛖᚾ ᚦᛖᚩ ᚺᚱᛖᚾᛋᛖᚺ ᚦᛖ

ᚠᚱᛖᛖᚹᚪᚩ? ᛋᛖᛖᚾ ᚦᚱᛁᛚᛚᛋ.

Hint: The first three words (which are shown above) are,
WHAT DID THE . . .

PIE-EYED

Grandma said she'd make her homemade cherry pie if you can figure out this problem: Given three bowls and 12 cherries, can you arrange the fruit so that there are an odd number of cherries in each bowl? Oh, and each bowl must contain more than three cherries.

Answer, page 373

JUMPER CABLES

In gym class, the teacher told a group of kids to each grab a jump rope from a pile. Which two kids are holding the same rope?

Answer, page 371

CATCH A CODE

Use the Morse code key to help you solve the coded message. The message is written without breaks between letters. When decoded, the dots and dashes will answer this question: What did the code inventor think when he had to repeat his message three times?

A • —   N — •
B — • • •   O — — —
C — • — •   P • — — •
D — • •   Q — — • —
E •   R • — •
F • • — •   S • • •
G — — •   T —
H • • • •   U • • —
I • •   V • • • —
J • — — —   W • — —
K — • —   X — • • —
L • — • •   Y — • — —
M — —   Z — — • •

MESSAGE: • • • • • • • — • • • — • • —
• — • • — — — — • — • • • • •

Answer, page 367

OUT OF SHAPE

The original shape below can be flipped and rotated in many ways. Which of the figures is not a rotated version of the original shape?

Answer, page 373

DOMINO EFFECT

Can you arrange the eight dominoes below to form a 4 x 4 square in which the number of pips in each row and column is the same? There is more than one answer.

Answer, page 368

TALK FOR A SPELL

Eight businesses in Centerville have phone numbers that spell out words appropriate for their services. Using the telephone number key, can you match each phone number to the business that uses it and name the word or words that each phone number stands for?

a. 356-9377   Travel agent
b. 967-5688   Coffee shop
c. 424-7288   Florist
d. 359-2929   Barber
e. 468-5282   Costume shop
f. 373-7787   Bank
g. 738-2273   Veterinarian
h. 728-3669   Health club

Answer, page 376

1	2 ABC	3 DEF
4 GHI	5 JKL	6 MNO
7 PRS	8 TUV	9 WXY

BEADY EYE

What number was added to the number on abacus A to get the total shown on abacus B?

Answer, page 367

A

B

SYMBOL MAZE

To solve this maze, you may move from one box to another only if they share a symbol. You will not use any symbol more than once. You may not move to any box that adjoins the box you are in (even diagonally). Start in the upper left corner and try to visit each box exactly once.

Answer, page 376

	A	B	C	D
1	☆ ○ ⊗	○ ✗ ←	∞ ▽ ⇔	⊗ ∞ ✦
2	≈ ∉ □	⇔ ⊃ ⊗	✗ ∉ ≈	⊃ ☆ ∞
3	○ ≈ ⬡	⬡ ⇔ ☆	▽ ← ⊃	← ∉ □

313

MATH MAZE

Begin with the number in the upper left square and travel to the lower right, calculating as you go. Can you find the solution path that meets the following restrictions?

- You may move to any adjacent (but not diagonal) square.
- You may not visit any square more than once.
- You must finish with the value shown in the last square.

Hint: No result along the way is a negative number or a fraction.

Answer, page 372

BEGIN

3	÷4	−1	×4	÷5
×2	−5	×3	−8	−2
×0	×7	÷2	+6	÷3
÷5	×6	+1	×5	+2
+8	÷4	+7	−9	=9

END

FIT TO BE TILED

Mrs. McGillicutty wants to put tile tops on two large tables. She wants to use tiles of either shape A or shape B. Each square in the tiles is one foot by one foot. The first table is eight by six feet and the second is eight by eight feet. Can you cover both tables according to her wishes without cutting any tiles?

Answer, page 369

A

B

RECEIPT DECEIT

The cash register printout at the Deuce hardware store isn't working very well. It is printing two sales on top of one another.

If Hank knows that one of his items cost $3.25, can you deduce the cost of his other purchases, his tax; and his total bill? Also, what were the amounts in the sale before his?

Answer, page 374

13.25

40.95

01.34

75.40   SUB

.35   TAX

75.75   TOT

THE GREAT PUMPKIN

Tom asked his mom for a recipe for pumpkin pie, because she makes great pies for the Elk's Club every year. Unfortunately, his mother uses a recipe for 80 pies.

If Tom has the ingredients that are listed, does he have enough to make two pies, based on the amounts from his mother's recipe?

MOM'S RECIPE
140 cups pumpkin
10   dozen eggs
120 cups evaporated milk
60   cups sugar
80   tsp. cinnamon

TOM'S PANTRY
4 cups pumpkin
2 eggs
3 cups evaporated milk
2 cups sugar
2 tsp. cinnamon

Answer, page 370

STARRY EYES

Can you find the one perfect, five-sided star in the field of shapes?

Answer, page 375

DRAW BY NUMBERS

Connect the points in the graph as directed. When you're done, you should see a familiar object.

Go from C10 to B10 to D13 to G14 to M14 to P13 to R10 to Q10 to P11 to N8 to N6 to P7 to Q7 to O4 to L5 to H5 to D1 to D2 to A5 to B6 to C5 to E5 to F9 to D11 to C10.
Then go from G9 to M9 to O12 to L13 to G13 to E12 to G9.

Answer, page 369

PIECES OF WISDOM

If you can put these jigsaw pieces together mentally, you will find part of a quote from Ralph Waldo Emerson describing what it is to be successful.

Answer, page 373

ZONED OUT

Amy is about to get on her flight to return home from Manila, and she wants to tell her boyfriend, Sheldon, when to pick her up at Kennedy airport. It is Thursday and her flight leaves at 4 p.m.

If New York is 11 hours behind the Philippines and Amy's flight time is 18 hours, plus an eight-hour layover in Hawaii, what day and time should Sheldon be waiting for her in New York?

Answer, page 377

THE PENNY FAIRY

Kelly rubbed her piggy bank and the Penny Fairy appeared. He told her she could choose her reward for freeing him. She could either have a ton of pennies or four miles of pennies lined up end to end. Which would you guess would be more money? Do some calculations to see if you are right.

Penny facts:
- One penny weighs about .0875 ounces.
- One penny is about .75 inches in diameter.

Answer, page 373

UNFOLDING MYSTERY

Two pieces of paper have been folded into fourths, and cutouts have been made in them as shown (1 and 2). What will the unfolded pieces look like (a, b, c, d, e, or f)?

Answer, page 377

PUZZLE PUZZLE

Every year for her birthday, Sandy gets a square jigsaw puzzle from her uncle. Each year, he finds a puzzle with more pieces than the last. This year, she received a 2,025-piece puzzle. How many edge pieces (including corners) should she look for?

     Also, Sandy's uncle has already bought next year's jigsaw puzzle, which has 204 edge pieces (including corners). How many total pieces does next year's puzzle have?

Answer, page 374

TAKE AIM

In a dart game of 201, players must throw exactly 201 points to win. They count backward, and must throw a double with their last dart.

All wedges count their face value. The small outer ring counts double and the small inner ring counts triple (the dart shows 3 x 7, or 21). The inner circle is 25 points and the bull's-eye is a double 25, or 50 points.

With three darts, it is possible to go out with as many as 170 points left (how?). And how would you go out if you had 164 points? 149 points?

Answer, page 376

325

MAKING FACES

At an unusual costume party, every guest is wearing a mask showing the face of another one of the guests. The name tags match the masks. Can you name all of the people under the false faces?

Answer, page 371

WALT WADE MIMI MONA

MAUDE BORIS VANCE MAX

GO FOR A SPIN

In each case, can you mentally rotate the wheels so that six three-letter words are spelled from the outside ring to the center? Hint: All of the words in each grid have something in common.

Answer, page 370

327

HAVE A HEART

All 13 hearts from a standard deck of cards are arranged here. Which one is face down?

Answer, page 370

SECRET WORDS

The first secret word has exactly two letters that are in each of these words:

    RIOT   WRAP
    CHEW   RACK
    COLD   GOWN

Can you name the word?

The second secret word has exactly two letters that are in each of these words:

    VIDEO   CURVY
    NORTH   HONEY
    SPARK   VALID

Can you name the second word?

Answer, page 374

PRETZEL LOGIC

Which of the pretzel pieces below comes from a bag of Mrs. Saline pretzels and which ones must have come from a different brand?

Answer, page 373

Mrs. Saline Pretzel:

STRIKE IT, RICH

Last Sunday, Rich bowled an almost perfect game. His friend Carl noticed that he knocked over the same number of pins as Rich but didn't score nearly as well. What are the two most divergent scores that can be bowled by knocking over the same number of pins?

Answer, page 376

SNACK ATTACK

Sally and Julie put their change together (shown below) and want to buy some snacks from the vending machines in their hotel. What can they afford to buy if they want to get two of each item?

- SODA: 65¢
- CHIPS: 80¢
- CANDY BAR: 50¢
- GUM: 45¢

Answer, page 375

CONCENTRATION

There are eight pairs of cards ranked 2 through 9 in this game of Concentration. Given the hints shown below and the two cards that are overturned, can you figure out where all of the pairs are?

1. No pairs appear in the same row or column.
2. No pairs appear in the same long diagonal.
3. The fourth column has only even numbers.
4. The second column has only odd numbers.
5. The first row contains the numbers 2 to 5.
6. The second row contains the numbers 6 to 9.
7. The corners contain the numbers 2 to 5.
8. There is a 3 in the upper left corner and a 4 in the lower right corner.

Answer, page 368

333

A WHALE'S TALE

Starting at the I in the upper left-hand corner, can you make knight's moves (see below) to jump to every square in the grid, without landing in any square twice, so that the letters you visit, in order, spell a phrase that tells you something about a blue whale's heart?

Answer, page 377

Knight's move

1		
		2

I	N	E	S	B
T	P	T	I	N
U	N	E	E	E
E	I	T	I	M
S	T	R	M	A

ORCHESTRATION

In the Pinedale Orchestra, there are 14 violinists and 8 cellists. Of those orchestra members, 5 belong to the Fencing Club and half are in the Snake Lovers Association. Of the 14 orchestra members in the clubs, only 2 belong to both, neither of whom are cellists. If 6 violinists are in neither club and 3 cellists are in the snake group, how many violinists are fencers? And how many cellists belong to neither club?

Answer, page 373

MILEAGE MILESTONES

Jean likes to take note of three mileage milestones on her odometer:

• Every time four of the same digits appear consecutively

• Every time the five-digit mileage is a palindrome (reads the same forward and backward)

• Every time the mileage is a "full house"; that is, two of one digit and three of another in any nonpalindromic order

One day, Jean noticed one milestone, noticed a second milestone 45 miles later, and a third milestone five miles after that. She noticed the third milestone again in one mile, followed by the second milestone in five miles and the first again in 45 miles. What were the mileage readings at each of those times?

Answer, page 372

GRILL SERGEANT

Joe is in charge of buying the food for his company picnic. Joe's butcher sells hot dogs in packages of 12. At the store, buns come in packages of eight, and paper plates are sold in multiples of 25. If Joe wants to use everything that he buys, with no leftovers, what is the fewest number of hot dogs that he has to grill?

Answer, page 370

CALENDAR GIRLS

Lydia and her friends are trying to find a good time for the next meeting of their investment club. Looking at next month, and the obligations that the five women already have, which weekday evening (or evenings) are possible meeting times?

- Lydia has volleyball games on Tuesdays and Thursdays.
- Sophie volunteers with Meals on Wheels every third day starting on the 1st.
- Daisy is busy every other Friday starting the 3rd and has tickets to concerts on the 15th and 29th.
- Fiona can't meet on Mondays and has book club on the 8th.

Answer, page 367

S	M	T	W	T	F	S
			1	2	3	4
5	6	7	8	9	10	11
12	13	14	15	16	17	18
19	20	21	22	23	24	25
26	27	28	29	30	31	

PUNCTUALITY

Can you add punctuation to make each of the following statements true?

1) she said two hundred and twenty is the product of two and ten and eleven is five plus six and also seven plus four

2) he jumped fifty times three is one hundred fifty over fifty four equals ninety less eighty six hundred is not a verb

Answer, page 373

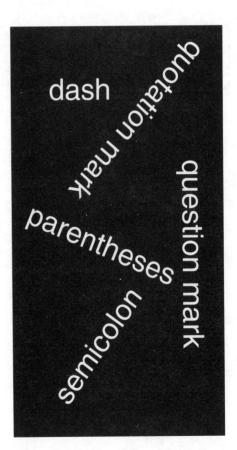

comma

hyphen

exclamation point

slash

colon

period

dash

quotation mark

parentheses

question mark

semicolon

ATTENTION, SHOPPERS

Lusina spent exactly $29 at a garage sale. If only the items shown were for sale, and she paid the prices as they are marked, what did she buy?

Answer, page 367

ATLAS $3

HAT $11

PICTURE $4

LAMP $7

MAILBOX $5

IRON $8

NUMBER LINES

Can you draw the straight line that passes through the highest number total for each box below?

Answer, page 372

A

B

THE RIGHT DIRECTION

Ray and Wendy were driving to a surprise party. Ray knew what part of town they were going to, but he couldn't find the house. They passed Owl Street and it started raining. By the time they drove by Rabbit Court for the third time, it was getting close to 12:00, when the surprise guest was to arrive. Ray asked to see the scrap of paper that the address was written on.

"Aha," he said, "Now I know what the problem is."
Do you?

Answer, page 374

WHAT'S THE BUZZ?

Locusts are a type of grasshopper that can travel in swarms of billions of insects and destroy crops. If one variety of plague locust appears every seven years and another variety appears every 12 years, and both types of locust hatched in the same year in 1957, when did (or when will) both varieties appear again in the same year? Also, in what year before 1957 did both types appear?

Answer, page 377

READY TO ROLL

One of the dice below is not a standard die. Which one is the fake?

Answer, page 374

A

B

C

D

E

MUDDLED

Each clue below can be answered with a five-letter word. In all, those words use only ten letters. One ten-letter word can be spelled using all those letters. Can you find it?

1. Be uncertain about
2. Make less blurry
3. Performed in a play
4. Sailing vessels
5. Huge meal
6. Chopped into dice-like pieces

Answer, page 372

ORDER, PLEASE

Ms. Carter, the homeroom teacher, lined up six students in the order shown by A. Not satisfied, she rearranged them in the order shown by B. What is the basis for each sequence?

Answer, page 373

	Arlene	Tyler	Barbara	Eric	Christie	Rob
A.	4	3	5	2	6	1
B.	4	1	3	5	6	2

GUESSTIMATION

Guess the number that correctly completes each statement below.

1. There are __ ridges on a quarter.
2. There are __ ridges on a dime.
3. You can fold a sheet of newspaper in half __ times.
4. There are ___ dimples on a golf ball.
5. There are __ letters in the Hawaiian alphabet.
6. You have to lick __ stamps to consume one calorie.
7. The average polar bear lives __ years.

a. 8
b. 10
c. 12
d. 20
e. 118
f. 119
g. 336

Answer, page 370

CIRCULAR NOTIONS

The circles below are hiding two interesting words. To find the words, start at the top letter in each case, and count clockwise a number of spaces (the number is for you to determine) to the next letter. Then, keep counting the same number of spaces and landing on a new letter until all the letters are used.

Answer, page 368

1.

"Burp"

2.

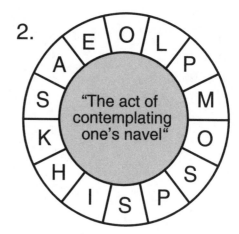

"The act of contemplating one's navel"

STICK HOUSES

In case A, can you move one stick and add another to create two matching houses?

Case B shows a farmer's pigpen. Can you move two fences and add two more to create two pigpens of the same shape and size?

Answer, page 376

A.

B.

CROSS WORDS

The words listed below fit into a grid so that each letter in the grid is used in one word reading across and one word reading down. Can you figure out the shape of the grid and how the words fit together?

Answer, page 368

ALONE	**GENIE**
ATONE	**MANIA**
DAM	**SAG**
DATES	**SALAD**
DEE	**SEA**

LED ASTRAY

The LED display on Art's calculator is malfunctioning. Only the top halves of the characters are showing. What equation is displayed below? If only the bottom halves of the display are showing, what are the two possibilities for the equation?

Answer, page 371

WHOA, BABY!

Jen gave birth to her daughter Caroline on the 1st of January in a year following a leap year. Starting in February, on the first of the month throughout that year, she made note of the day of the week. She noticed that the monthly anniversary of her daughter's birth fell on a Friday three times that year. On what day of the week was Caroline born? And how many months old was Caroline before her monthly "birthday" fell on its original day for the third time (not counting her actual day of birth)?

Answer, page 377

SKETCH PAD

Al came across these two Etch A Sketch drawings in a toy store. Can you figure out how someone drew each shape using one continuous line, not retracing any part of either figure?

Answer, page 375

LETTER CODES

The code below hides two nonsense sentences.
Only the ten most common letters in English are used in the codes. The most common letter appears ten times, the next most common appears nine times, etc. What are the two sentences and what are the ten most frequently used letters in English?

1. Q UWGZW G BWGU GBUWGUWX QB

    GZQG.

2. ZWW, QU'Z UPP JPU UP JPPU QB

    WXQW—JWGK PB.

Answer, page 371

ABCDEFGHIJKLMNOPQRSTUVWXYZ

REBUS RIDDLES

Add and subtract the letters of the illustrated words as indicated to find the answers to the riddles.

Answer, page 374

1. What has a head but no eyes?

2. What has an eye but no head?

PICTURE THIS

When overlapped, the lines on the two squares below will form a picture. Can you figure out which way to rotate the squares and what appears in the combined image? The squares do not need to be flipped over, and they should be rotated in 90-degree increments.

Answer, page 373

A.

B.

NOTE WORTHY

Even if you can't read music, you might be able to identify the children's songs below from their first few notes.

Answer, page 372

Hint: The last word of the first song bite is "are" and the first word of the second song is "I've."

SPILLED MILK

It was one o'clock when Randy put on a freshly laundered pair of pants. His roommate asked him if he'd go buy some milk, and gave him a $5 bill. When Randy got back from the store, he put his change down on the counter and told his roommate that he'd also bought some chips at the grocery store, which he'd eaten on the way home. His roommate didn't believe him. Why?

Answer, page 375

IT TAKES ALL SORTS

Kevin likes the opera but not the ballet. He has a boxer but won't get a bulldog. He will travel to Colorado but not Alaska. He collects dimes but not nickels. Does he like bananas or grapes?

Rhonda will go see ballet but not opera. Her favorite number is eight and she doesn't like nine. She likes salmon but not trout. She hates Mondays but likes Wednesdays. Does she use a comb or a brush?

Answer, page 371

COMPUTER LANGUAGE

The binary code below represents a joke and its answer. Given that each letter is represented by a string of eight 0s and/or 1s, can you break the code?

01010111010010000100010101010011100101101001000101010101001
00100111101010000010011000100000101011001010001010010001
00010100110100111101000011010000110100010101010010010101010
11101001001010101000100100001001111010011100100010101010010
01110100100001000001010101000100100001000001010100000010
1000001000101010011100100010101010000100?

01011010010001010101001001001001111010101110100111101001110
0010011110100111001000101010110100100010101010010010011
11.

Answer, page 368

Hint: The first word is "when."

THE CHIPS ARE DOWN

A black cat just knocked all of the chips off of Grandma's bingo card. And she was so close to BINGO, too. There were only five open squares on her card, and yet not one full row or column.

   If there were no 2s showing and G55 was uncovered, can you put the chips back on the card to show how it looked before the cat stepped on it?

Answer, page 368

B	I	N	G	O
8	16	43	55	61
13	29	37	56	70
5	24	free	48	72
14	19	35	59	67
1	23	42	50	71

OUT ON A LIMB

Henry has started a calorie-counting diet. He wants to burn exactly as many calories as he consumes, and his favorite form of exercise is climbing trees. Given that his breakfast of one dozen doughnuts has cost him 2,700 calories, and that he wants to climb all of these trees at least once, how many of each tree should Henry climb before lunch?

Answer, page 373

MAPLE: 120

REDWOOD: 530

OAK: 210

GONE TO PIECES

Only ten pieces remain in your animal cracker box, below.
What animals were they?

Answer, page 370

PHONE-Y WORDS

Each number in the grid below stands for one of three letters, as shown on the telephone buttons. Four four-letter words read across and four four-letter words read down. Each number stands for a different letter reading across than down. What unique set of common, uncapitalized words will fill the grid?

Answer, page 373

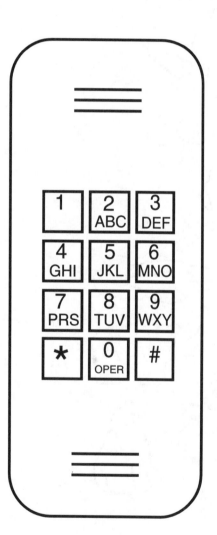

8	4	5	9
3	6	6	3
2	2	6	3
5	4	2	7

SEEDS OF DOUBT

Early this spring, Mrs. Rowe planted a 3 x 4–square foot garden with six different vegetables. Now, a few sprouts are coming up, but she doesn't remember where the potatoes are.

Using the clues and the map of the garden, can you figure out which squares hold potatoes?

1. Each vegetable uses a 2 x 1-foot plot of adjacent squares.
2. Spinach has sprouted in A1.
3. Cucumbers are coming up in A2.
4. Basil is budding in B2.
5. Every plant in column C is different.
6. Peas are popping up in C3.
7. Onions are on their way in D3.

Answer, page 374

	A	B	C	D
1				
2				
3				

CLOCK WISE

While staying at a friend's house, you notice that there are three clocks in the bedroom, but they all show different times.

When you ask your friend for the correct time, he yells from the kitchen, "One clock is 20 minutes fast, one is slow, and one is off by 30 minutes, but I forget in which direction."

What time is it?

Answer, page 368

Answers

Ages of Reason (page 280)
Aunt Pearl is 64 years old (LXIV) and her daughter is 46 (XLVI). The numbers 66 (LXVI) and 44 (XLIV) can also be made from the same symbols.

Alligator Ally (page 302)
The alligator is on the left and is lying.

Animal Strength (page 253)
The frogs will win the third tug of war. Two turtles will tie with four frogs.

Attention, Shoppers (page 340)
Lusina bought the atlas, hat, lamp, and iron.

Beady Eye (page 312)
8,888 was added to abacus A (8,375) to get the sum on abacus B (17,263).

Berry Impressive (page 278)
There will be 34 strawberries at the beginning of November. The number of berries each month is the famous Fibonacci sequence (1, 1, 2, 3, 5, 8, ...), where each number is the sum of the previous two.

Black and White (page 281)
1. You have two white cards.
2. You have one white card and one black card. (If you had two black cards, A would know what he had on the second round, because if he had two of the same card, one of you would have seen four of one color and known you had two of the other color.)

Blind Alleys (page 263)
They started in Redland.

Block Party (page 260)
She took the "CUBE ROUTE."

Calendar Girls (page 338)
The only day that works for everyone is Friday the 24th.

Catch a Code (page 308)
HE FELT REMORSE (re"Morse.")

Categorically Speaking (page 296)

	S	C	A	M	P
Girls' names:	Scarlet	Candy	Amber	Myrtle	Pearl
Colors:	sand	coral	amethyst	magenta	purple
Trees:	spruce	chestnut	apple	mango	palm
Flowers:	snowball	camellia	amaryllis	magnolia	primrose
On a beach:	shell	chair	anemone	mussel	pail

The Chips Are Down (page 361)

Circular Notions (page 348)

1. ERUCTATION (count seven squares at a time)
2. OMPHALOSKEPSIS (count three squares at a time)

Clock Wise (page 366)

It is 9:45.

Coffee Break (page 293)

A cup of tea has one-half the caffeine of a cup of coffee, and two times the caffeine of a can of cola.

Computer Language (page 360)

The code says, "When zero played soccer with one what happened? Zero won one zero."

Concentration (page 333)

Cross Words (page 350)

```
    S A G
  D A T E S
  A L O N E
  M A N I A
    D E E
```

Detective Story (page 292)

Slooth should arrest the man in the Civic. Chiller is calling from Thunder Bay, Ontario, where they measure the temperature in Celsius. Thirty degrees Celsius is 86 degrees Fahrenheit.

Domino Effect (page 310)

Rotations of this arrangement also work.

Draw by Numbers (page 319)

Familiar Faces (page 291)

All of the coins are correct except for the dime.

Fishing for Words (page 272)

The proverb reads, "The fish dies because he opens his mouth."

Fishing Lines (page 279)

Fit for a Princess (page 298)

The princess can wear four combinations of one piece of jewelry, six combinations of two, four combinations of three, and one combination of all four jewels, for a total of 15 different combinations.

Fit to Be Tiled (page 315)

The 8 x 8 table can be covered with shape B (but not shape A). The 8 x 6 table can be covered with shape A (but not shape B).

For Your Thoughts (page 283)

1. A
2. C

Fraction Words (page 267)

A. Florida (fl + or + ida)
B. piano (pi + an + o)

Game Plan (page 284)

A: Player X wins; B: Player X wins (X plays above O first, then no matter where O plays, X can either win on the next turn or take the lowest empty right-hand box and win on the following turn).

Get the Scoop (page 297)

The free ice cream will be on the first Tuesday in July.

Give Me Five (page 303)

These are our answers (there may be others):
$(3 \times 3 + 3 + 3) \div 3 = 5$
$(4 - 4 + 4) \div 4 + 4 = 5$
$5 - 5 + 5 - 5 + 5 = 5$
$6 - (6 \div 6) + (6 - 6) = 5$
$7 - (7 \div 7) - (7 \div 7) = 5$
$8 - [(8 + 8) \div 8] = 5$
$[(9 \times 9) + 9] \div (9 + 9) = 5$

Global Economy (page 300)

The best deal is in Sweden, where the CD costs an equivalent of $9 U.S.

Go for a Spin (page 327)

1: jaw, ear, hip, toe, arm, and leg.
2: ape, gnu, pig, elk, fox, and yak.

Gone to Pieces (page 363)

1. alligator; 2. giraffe; 3. gorilla; 4. whale; 5. whale; 6. seal; 7. gorilla; 8. elephant; 9. zebra; 10. rhinoceros.

A Good Egg (page 276)

1. T; 2. W; 3. E; 4. L; 5. V; 6. E. An ostrich egg equals about 24 hen's eggs, or 12 omelets.

Got Class? (page 273)

This class schedule will work: Biology, European history, Genetics, Shakespeare, and Statistics.

Graphic Language (page 264)

Because seven eight nine ("seven ate nine").

The Great Pumpkin (page 317)

Tom has enough of everything except eggs. He will need one more egg to make two pies.

Grill Sergeant (page 337)

To use everything that he buys, Joe must grill at least 600 hot dogs (50 packages of dogs, 75 packages of buns, and 24 packages of plates). Any multiple of 600 will also come out even.

Guesstimation (page 347)

1. f; 2. e; 3. a; 4. g; 5. c; 6. b; 7. d.

Hairy Tales (page 258)

1. Rapunzel was trapped for 200 years.
2. Rip Van Winkle's beard should have been ten feet long.

Have a Heart (page 328)

The 10 of hearts is face down.

Hula Hoopla (page 304)

The equations represent these numbers: 1. $2 \times 2 + 5 = 9$; 2. $8 \div 4 \times 2 = 4$; 3. $9 \div 3 + 3 = 6$; 4. $2 + 6 - 3 = 5$ or e'lima.

Irish Eyes (page 287)

It's About Time (page 290)

1. B (7–11); 2. D (9 to 5); 3. E (737); 4. A (1040); 5. C (5' 10"); 6. F (101).

It Takes All Sorts (page 359)

Kevin likes bananas. He likes words that alternate vowels and consonants, like his name. Rhonda uses a comb. She likes words that have silent letters, like her name.

Jollos and Plotz (page 289)

Jollos have a circle, triangle, and two lines; plotz have a circle and four lines. A and C are plotz.

Jumper Cables (page 307)

Stan and Jan are grabbing the same rope.

Keep the Faith (page 259)

Old Faithful's next eruption will be at 4:50 P.M. The formula used to figure out the time until the next eruption is 4D + 30 minutes, where D is the duration of the last eruption.

Key Rings (page 288)

A. yes
B. no (two groups of two are connected)
C. yes

LED Astray (page 351)

Top portion showing: 73 + 19 = 92.
Lower portion showing: 45 + 18 = 63 or 49 + 16 = 65.

Letter Codes (page 354)

1. I tease a neat anteater in Asia.
2. See, it's too hot to hoot in Erie—head on.
The ten most common letters, in order of use, are: e, t, a, o, i, n, s, h, r, and d.

Losing Track (page 262)

Deb cheated. The answers are: 1. bison; 2. caribou; 3. deer; 4. moose; 5. mountain goat.

Making Faces (page 326)

From left to right from the top: Max, Maude, Wade, Walt, Vance, Mona, Mimi, and Boris.

Match Boxes (page 275)

Only piece e will not form a box.

Math Maze (page 314)

Mileage Milestones (page 336)

49,949; 49,994; 49,999; 50,000; 50,005; and 50,050.

Mind Boggler (page 250)

The numbers ONE through TEN can be spelled by moving from letter to adjacent letter. THREE is the only number that cannot be spelled (without using the same E two times in a row).

Mirror Images (page 271)

Figures four and seven are impossible with just one mirror.

Muddled (page 345)

1. doubt; 2. focus; 3. acted; 4. boats; 5. feast; 6. cubed. The ten-letter word is OBFUSCATED.

Next in Line (page 274)

Each item is spelled with all the letters from the one before, plus one: TEA, TAPE, PLEAT, and STAPLE. The next item in the sequence is PLANETS (a).

Note Worthy (page 357)

1. "Twinkle, Twinkle, Little Star" (or "The Alphabet Song")
2. "I've Been Working on the Railroad"

Novel Idea (page 301)

1. AUTHRSAREALL
2. AWHRSAREALL
3. AWHRSAREALLDD
4. AWHRSARETHEALLDD
5. AWHRSARETHEALNLDND
6. AWHRSIATRETHEALNLDND
7. AWHRSIATRETHEALNLDMEND
8. WRITEHANDED
9. WRITE HANDED

Number Lines (page 341)

A. 35; B. 44.

Orchestration (page 335)

Two violinists are fencers (they are also in the snake club). Two cellists are in neither group.

Order, Please (page 346)

In the first case, the kids are in order of the length of their first names; in the second, the names form a chain in which the last letter of each name is the first letter of the next.

Out of Shape (page 309)

B, F, G, and I are not versions of the original shape.

Out on a Limb (page 362)

Henry should climb four maples, three redwoods, and three oaks before lunch.

Paper Clip Flip (page 255)

Number 1 is shorter than the original. Numbers 3 and 10 are longer than the original.

Paper Pinball (page 295)

10, +20, −5, +10, +15, +5, +10, −10, +15, +10, +5, +40, −20, +25, +40, −5, +10, −10, +25, +5, +15, −5, +30, −10, +15, +30, +20, +5 = 295.

The Penny Fairy (page 322)

Four miles of pennies equals $3,379.20; one ton equals $3,657.14. The ton is $277.94 more.

Phone-y Words (page 364)

Across: ugly, food, band, liar.
Down: teak, inch, knob, weep.

Picture This (page 356)

Pieces of Wisdom (page 320)

"To laugh often and much."

Pie-Eyed (page 306)

Here's one answer: Put five cherries in one bowl, five cherries in another, and put one of those inside the third bowl, which holds two cherries.

Pretzel Logic (page 330)

Pieces two and eight are not Mrs. Saline pretzels.

Produce Products (page 265)

The equations are: 9 − 3 = 6; 4 x 2 = 8; 1 + 4 = 5; and 6 ÷ 3 = 2. Therefore, the carrot is 7.

Punctuality (page 339)

1) She said, "two hundred." And twenty is the product of two and ten. And eleven is five plus six and also seven plus four.
2) He jumped fifty times. Three is one hundred fifty over fifty. Four equals ninety less eighty-six. "Hundred" is not a verb.

Puzzle Puzzle (page 324)

This year's puzzle has 176 edge pieces (45 per side—the corner pieces are part of two sides). Next year's puzzle has 2,704 total pieces.

Ready to Roll (page 344)

Die D is not a standard die (all pairs of numbers on opposite sides should add up to seven).

Rebus Riddles (page 355)

1. bead + rug + stem – bag – tees = drum
2. stork + nail + radio – ski – rail = tornado

Receipt Deceit (page 316)

Hank's purchases were 3.25 + 0.75 + 1.30 = 5.30 + .25 tax = $5.55. The sale before his was for 1.80 + 4.96 + 0.64 = 7.40 + .35 tax = $7.75.

The Right Direction (page 342)

Wendy was looking at the scrap of paper upside down. They should have been looking for 819 Pooh. Ray recognized that Owl Street and Rabbit Court were part of the same Winnie-the-Pooh–themed neighborhood.

Ruff and Ready (page 299)

There were 28 people and 35 dogs.

Runed Punch Line (page 305)

What did the chickens get when they crossed the freeway? Cheep thrills.

Sea or Soil? (page 277)

The treasure is buried underwater.

Secret Words (page 329)

The first word is CROW; the second word is RAVEN.

Seeds of Doubt (page 365)

The potatoes are in squares C1 and D1.

Self Test (page 261)

1. 8; 2. 6; 3. 4; 4. 1; 5. 9; 6. 7; 7. 5; 8. 3; 9. 2.

Shifting Gears (page 285)

1. clockwise; 2. clockwise; 3. counterclockwise; 4. these gears won't turn.

Sketch Pad (page 353)

1. Start at the top of the three circles. Go around the first circle counterclockwise, then out across the top of the topmost bar and back across the bottom of it. Then go around the center circle counterclockwise, out across the top of the second (left-pointing) bar and back across the bottom of it. Finish by going around the bottom circle counterclockwise, out across the top of the lowest bar and back across the bottom of it. There are several variations that will work.

2. Start on the leftmost vertical line at its center point. Trace the upper left-hand square going counterclockwise. Then go three-quarters of the way around the bottom left square, also counterclockwise. Now angle down and to the right, back left, up and to the right, up and to the left, across to the right, down and to the left, across to the right, and down. Next move three-quarters of the way around the bottom right square, counterclockwise, then finish up the upper right-hand square in a clockwise direction. Again, there are several variations.

Slice of Life (page 282)

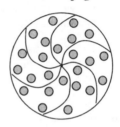

Snack Attack (page 332)

The girls have $2.30. They can buy two sodas and two candy bars.

Spilled Milk (page 358)

Randy had more than a dollar in change, so he must have gone to more than one store.

Starry Eyes (page 318)

375

Stick Houses (page 349)

Strike It, Rich (page 331)

Rich had 11 strikes in a row, but threw a gutter ball on the last ball of the 10th frame for 290 points in 110 pins. Carl hit 110 pins by throwing a gutter ball followed by a spare (all 10 pins) in the first 10 frames and a strike on the bonus ball of the 10th frame, for a total of 110 points—a difference of 180 points.

Symbol Maze (page 313)

Starting with the circle: A1, A3, C2, A2, D3, B1, D1, B2, D2, B3, C1, and C3.

Take Aim (page 325)

Triple 20, triple 20, bull's-eye = 170. Triple 19, triple 19, bull's-eye = 164. Triple 20, triple 19, double 16 = 149. (Other possibilities exist for 164 and 149.)

Talk for a Spell (page 311)

a-florist (FLOWERS); b-health club (WORKOUT); c-barber (HAIRCUT); d-travel agent (FLY AWAY); e-coffee shop (HOT JAVA); f-costume shop (DRESS UP); g-veterinarian (PET CARE); h-bank (SAVE NOW).

Technique-Color (page 252)

Piece A should be orange.

Ten Gold Coins (page 270)

Theory of Relativity (page 254)

You are Bernie.

Thirteen Candles (page 257)

The candles form 50 triangles: 18 made by the six points around the edge; 18 using the full side of the two large triangles; 12 made of half of a full side; and 2 large triangles.

Three Hexes (page 268)

Numbers three and seven are made with four hexagons.

To the Letter (page 286)

In order, the letters spell "verbatim."

Tough Cookies (page 294)

There were 36 cookies on the plate.

12-Step Program (page 256)

The output reads: BOOT UP.

Tying the Knot (page 251)

She should start her subscription to *Brides* magazine. Ropes 1, 2, and 5 will form knots.

Unfolding Mystery (page 323)

1 matches a and 2 matches f.

A Whale's Tale (page 334)

The phrase is: It beats nine times per minute.

What's the Buzz? (page 343)

The two varieties of locusts appear together every 84 years: 1873, 1957, and 2041.

What's the Plan? (page 266)

Object one fits the plan.

Whoa, Baby! (page 352)

Caroline was born on a Tuesday. She was 18 months old when her "birthday" fell on a Tuesday for the third time (in her second July).

Winter Eyes (page 269)

A–1; B–7; C–4.

Zoned Out (page 321)

Assuming her plane is on time, Amy will arrive at Kennedy airport at 7 a.m. on Friday.

Index

All puzzles are indexed by page number

WHAT IS MENSA?

Mensa®
The High IQ Society

Mensa is the international society for people with a high IQ. We have more than 100,000 members in over 40 countries worldwide.

The society's aims are:
- to identify and foster human intelligence for the benefit of humanity;
- to encourage research in the nature, characteristics, and uses of intelligence;
- to provide a stimulating intellectual and social environment for its members.

Anyone with an IQ score in the top two percent of the population is eligible to become a member of Mensa—are you the "one in 50" we've been looking for?

Mensa membership offers an excellent range of benefits:
- Networking and social activities nationally and around the world;
- Special Interest Groups (hundreds of chances to pursue your hobbies and interests—from art to zoology!);
- Monthly International Journal, national magazines, and regional newsletters;
- Local meetings—from game challenges to food and drink;
- National and international weekend gatherings and conferences;
- Intellectually stimulating lectures and seminars;
- Access to the worldwide SIGHT network for travelers and hosts.

For more information about Mensa International:
www.mensa.org
Telephone: +44 20 7226 6891
e-mail: enquiries@mensa.org
Mensa International Ltd.
P.O. Box 215
Lowestoft, NR32 9BD
United Kingdom

For more information about American Mensa:
www.us.mensa.org
Telephone: 1-800-66-MENSA
American Mensa Ltd.
1229 Corporate Drive West
Arlington, TX 76006-6103
USA

For more information about British Mensa (UK and Ireland):
www.mensa.org.uk
Telephone: +44 (0) 1902 772771
e-mail: enquiries@mensa.org.uk
British Mensa Ltd.
St. John's House
St. John's Square
Wolverhampton WV2 4AH
United Kingdom

For more information about Australian Mensa:
www.mensa.org.au
Telephone: +61 1902 260 594
e-mail: info@mensa.org.au
Australian Mensa Inc.
PO Box 212
Darlington WA 6070
Australia